CLASSIFICATION MADE SIMPLE

Classification Made Simple

Second edition

ERIC J. HUNTER

ASHGATE

Published by
Ashgate Publishing Limited
Gower House,
Croft Road,
Aldershot,
Hampshire GU11 3HR
England

Ashgate Publishing Company
Suite 420
101 Cherry Street
Burlington, VT 05401-4405
USA

First published 1988
Second edition 2002
Reprinted 2005

Ashgate website: http://www.ashgate.com

British Library Cataloguing-in-Publication Data
Hunter, Eric J. (Eric Joseph), 1930-
   Classification made simple. - 2nd ed.
   1. Classification - Books
   I. Title
   025.4'2

Library of Congress Control Number: 2001099658

ISBN 0 7546 0795 X

Printed and bound in Great Britain by MPG Books Ltd, Bodmin, Cornwall

Contents

Acknowledgements

The author wishes to express his appreciation for the willing assistance given by a number of people from various organizations and institutions, including: Eric Coates (BSO); Cheryl Cook (Library of Congress); Gillian Dwyer and Penny Camm-Jones (London Business School); Ken Linkman (University of Liverpool); Claudia Merrick (RIBA); Richard Moore (British Library); Peter Moss (London Institute of Education Library); and Professor Mohinder Satija (Guru Nanak Dev University, India). Thanks are also due to ex-colleagues on the staff of Liverpool John Moores University for their help with the first edition.

E.J.H.

Introduction

This brief work was written in an attempt to simplify the initial study of classification as used for information retrieval.

The text adopts a gradual progression from very basic principles, a progression that, hopefully, will enable the reader to gain a firm grasp of one idea before proceeding to the next. Practical examples are provided as illustration and reinforcement at each stage.

It must, however, be stressed that the work constitutes an elementary, introductory study only; as such it should provide a gateway to more advanced treatises and more detailed studies of specific schemes.

In information work, classification may be used in various ways, for coding in computerized systems; for the organization of manual and machine-readable files and catalogues; and for shelf arrangement in libraries and information services. It can constitute a basis for the production of alphabetical authority lists of subject terms, or thesauri, and can be applied to other subject indexing and search techniques. The approach adopted here is a wide one and is not limited to classification for one specific purpose.

This revision takes account of developments that have taken place since the first edition was published. For example, a 21st edition of the *Dewey Decimal Classification* was published in 1996, the *CI/SfB Construction Indexing Manual* was superseded by *Uniclass* in 1997 and a new edition of the *London Classification of Business Studies* appeared in 2000. Machine-readable versions of schemes such as *Dewey* and the *Library of Congress Classification* have been prepared and the latter classification and other schemes, such as the *ACM Computing Classification System,* are also available on the Internet. The phenomenal growth of the 'net and the World Wide Web has been one of the most significant events of recent years and this new edition includes an additional chapter that outlines the significant role that classification can play in the accessing of Internet resources.

1   What is Classification?

Consider the following images:

Could you tell the difference? Certainly you could; you would be in a certain amount of trouble if you couldn't. This means that you are capable of carrying out a process of *classification.*

In essence the process of classification simply means the grouping together of like things according to some common quality or characteristic. This automatically implies the separation of the unlike as in the above example.

As human beings we are able to recognize a member of a particular class because it displays certain characteristics common to that class but not to others. Examine the following collection:

From observation one is able immediately to identify like entities:

Forms of transport   **Means of communication**

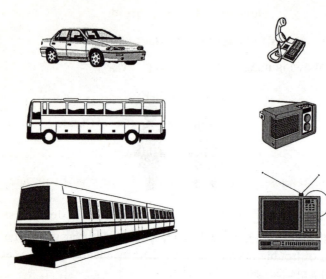

In making the above distinction and grouping the things as shown, a process of classification has been carried out in that like things have been grouped together and unlike things separated.   It is essential for a person to be able to think logically in this way and to make such distinctions – classification 'lies at the base of every well-managed life and occupation' (Maltby, 1975).   Otherwise one would be sitting on the television set waiting to be transported to work! Beam me up, Scotty!

Wherever one looks, examples of the use of classification can be found. Take, for instance, the case of Harrison Ford, alias Indiana Jones.   Ford hasn't always been a film actor.   In the early 1970s he became seriously dissatisfied with the sameness and blandness of the work that he was being offered so he gave up acting and became a carpenter instead (Norman, 1997).   Apparently he became a very good carpenter and examples of his work are to be found to this day in many a home in Beverly Hills (*ibid.*). When Ford was whittling wood, he kept all of his carpentry tools laid out in order of type and size right though his entire workshop (Courtenay, 1994).   He realized that this would make his work that much easier.   By putting all of his *cutting* tools together, Ford would separate them immediately from his *drilling* tools and from his *smoothing* tools. Clearly, he recognizes the enormous value of classification.

What would Ford have to say, do you think, if he visited his local supermarket and found the goods arranged as shown below?

Liqueurs   Lamb   Bread

Beans   Margarine   Wine   Potatoes

Cakes   Beer   Beef   Tea

Spirits   Butter

Cabbage   Pies   Carrots   Coffee   Cheese

Pork   Cocoa   Chicken

It would be **chaos**!   Shopping would be very difficult and time consuming.

No doubt Ford would much prefer, as we all would, to find similar products shelved together and differing products separated:

Lamb	Bread	Liqueurs	Beans	Tea	Margarine
Beef	Cakes	Wine	Potatoes	Coffee	Butter
Pork	Pies	Beer	Cabbage	Cocoa	Cheese
Chicken		Spirits	Carrots		

Classification makes shopping, and indeed all aspects of our lives, very much easier.

References

Courtenay, Chris (1994), 'Indiana Jones and his homely crusade', *Daily Mail Weekend* (16 July), pp. 4-5.

Maltby, Arthur (1975), *Sayers' Manual of Classification for Librarians*, 5th edn, Deutsch, London, p. 15.

Norman, Barry (1997), 'Why Ford sticks to what he does best', *Radio Times* (12-18 April), p. 46.

2   Classification in an Information System

Specifically — from the point of view of this book — classificatory techniques may be applied in an information and retrieval system in order to facilitate access to, and use of, the system. The information system could be a manual office filing system or a computerized data processing system, in which classification might be employed for coding entities. Where the recent phenomenon of the Internet is concerned, search engines and other facilities also make use of classification. In fact, it can be demonstrated, as we shall see, that whatever method of indexing or retrieval is used, just as in life itself, classification cannot be ignored.

Probably the most common example of a system that makes use of classification is the library or information service, where classification by subject is extensively used to arrange books and other materials on the shelves or to make entries for them in catalogues and indexes. If, for instance, we visited the local public library we would find the sciences:

Mathematics
Astronomy
Physics
Chemistry
Geology

shelved adjacent to each other, brought together by the classification scheme in use (possibly the *Dewey Decimal Classification* or *Library of Congress Classification*).

In Chapter 1 mention was made of Harrison Ford giving up acting at one time. After he took this step, 'He joined the local library to read up on carpentry and woodwork . . . before proceeding to totally strip and gut his home from top to bottom . . . and rebuild the entire house to his own specification' (Sellers, 1993). When first he was shown where the carpentry books where located on the library shelves, he found them nestling amongst other works which might also be of use to him — books on bricklaying, plastering, plumbing and so on. Again, these related subjects had been brought together by means of *classification*.

Subjects

The reader may have noted that the 'things' listed on page 2 are all concrete entities, whilst sciences such as 'mathematics' involve abstract ideas. For example, a television is concrete but the activity of insuring the television against theft is abstract. In this text, for simplicity, both concrete entities and abstract ideas, or combinations of both (for example open-heart surgery), will usually be referred to as subjects.

Complexity of subjects

In an information system a classification scheme must not only cater for simple subjects which consist of a single concept, for example:

> **Sex**
> **Children**
> **Psychology**
> **Teaching**
> **Steel**
> **Wires**
> **Plating**

but also for more complex subjects which are formed by combining these concepts, for example:

> **Psychology of sex**
> **Child psychology**
> **Teaching children about sex**
> **Teaching psychology**
> **Teaching child psychology**
> **Steel wires**
> **Plating steel wires**

In order to achieve this objective the system of classification, as used in an information system, may adopt a 'hierarchical' or 'faceted' approach, or a mixture of both. The former, as the name implies, utilizes a 'top down' approach, a process of division producing a series of subject classes in successive subordination. Faceted classification, on the other hand, makes use of a 'bottom up' technique, constituent parts of subjects being used as nuts and bolts to produce whatever subject classes are required.

The subject 'Wood finishing', for example, could be divided hierarchically by process. Each process would be further subdivided. It might be thought suitable to divide 'staining' by the 'type' of stain, for example 'dyes' and the 'type' of stain by 'shade': 'mahogany', 'oak', 'teak' and so on, as shown below for 'Water stains'.

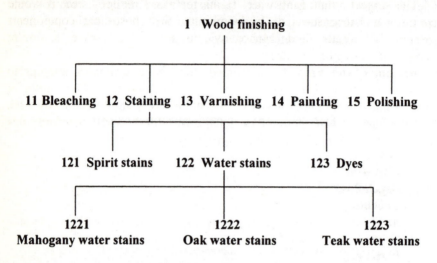

Thus the subject 'Mahogany water stains for wood' is listed within the hierarchy and would be classified as 1221.

A faceted classification, on the other hand, would simply list within facets, or 'groups', the terms that together make up the subject, for example:

1 Wood finishing

Process facet
   1 Bleaching
   2 Staining
   3 Varnishing
   4 Painting
   5 Polishing

Type facet
   1 Spirit
   2 Water
   3 Dye

Shade facet
1 Mahogany
2 Oak
3 Teak

The subject 'Mahogany water stains for wood' is not listed; it would have to be 'reconstructed' by combining the constituent components 'Staining', 'Water' and 'Mahogany', to give, in this case, a similar classification number — 1221.

Although only partially developed, the above examples attempt to illustrate the basic difference between the two methods. The nature of faceted classification enables it 'to be more easily interpretable by both human beings and computers' (Clifton, 1994) and therefore this methodology will be the first to be more fully described.

References

Clifton, H.O. and Sutcliffe, A.G. (1994), *Business Information Systems*, 5th edn, Prentice Hall, London; New York, p. 320.
Sellers, Robert (1993), *Harrison Ford: a Biography*, Hale, London, p. 33.

3 Faceted Classification

A facet is defined in the Oxford Dictionary as 'one side of a many sided body'. Subjects can be broken down into constituent sides or parts and the word faceted, as we saw in Chapter 2, may therefore be applied to a classification which works on an analytico-synthetic principle. Fundamental concepts are analysed and grouped together into facets. These concepts can then be combined or synthesized as necessary to form more complex subjects. The following further example should help to make this principle clearer.

A United Kingdom brewing company sells canned and bottled beers (mild, bitter, lager, and stout) in various sizes from 330 ml to 3½ litres. The company wishes to devise a faceted classification scheme for coding items in its computerized sales system. In order to do this the relevant concepts, '330 ml', 'cans', 'bitter' and so on, are grouped into facets using the characteristics of 'capacity', 'container' and 'beer type', that is:

Capacity facet	Container facet	Beer type facet
330 ml	Cans	Mild
440 ml	Bottles	Bitter
550 ml		Lager
1 litre		Stout
3½ litre		

Notation

Each concept within the classification scheme must be allocated a notational symbol which will enable the representation of that concept by a 'shorthand' code or classification number. Numeric digits could perform this function. Here is such a notation added to the above scheme:

Capacity facet		Container facet		Beer type facet	
1	330 ml	1	Cans	1	Mild
2	440 ml	2	Bottles	2	Bitter
3	550 ml			3	Lager
4	1 litre			4	Stout
5	3½ litre				

The process of classification

The process of classification is achieved by first ascertaining the notation for each constituent concept and then combining (synthesizing) these notations to form a coding or classification number for the complete subject. For example, to classify '440 ml cans of lager' the subject is first broken down into its constituent concepts:

440 ml   cans   lager

and the relevant notations ascertained from the classification scheme:

2   1   3

These separate notations are then combined or synthesized to give the classification number:

213

Similarly:

1 litre bottles of mild   = **421**
3½ litre cans of bitter   = **512**

In order to avoid confusion, when using a notation such as that shown here, the notational length (that is the number of digits) must be constant and concepts from facets must be combined or cited in a consistent order. In the above examples the order is that in which the facets have been written down, namely:

Capacity → Container → Type of beer

If a coding in a computerized system were all that was required, then the above scheme would be satisfactory, but for other purposes, for example a manual filing system, it would be inadequate. The reasons for this are explained at a later point in this text (page 16).

The initial steps involved in compiling a faceted scheme

Let us now review the steps that have been taken in order to compile the faceted scheme.

Step 1   Analysis into relevant concepts, that is:

440 ml
bitter
cans
lager
1 litre
etc

Step 2   Grouping into facets according to appropriate characteristics, for example:

Capacity facet	Container facet	Beer type facet
440 ml	Cans	Bitter
1 litre	Bottles	Lager
etc		

Step 3   Adding a notation, for example:

2   440 ml
4   1 litre
    etc

Step 4   Choosing a citation order, for example:

Capacity → Container → Type of beer

A further decision, which has not been specifically referred to, also had to be taken. This relates to the way in which the scheme is to be written down or printed, that is the schedule order. In the above example the schedule order is:

Capacity → Container → Type of beer

(which is the same as the citation order but it need not necessarily be so; this point is explained more fully later - page 77). Schedule order would therefore become Step 5:

Step 5   Deciding upon the schedule order

For very brief schedules a tabular form of presentation can be used, as shown on page 8, but for lengthier schemes a continuous form is more appropriate, for example:

Capacity facet
1   300 ml
2   440 ml
3   550 ml
4   1 litre
5   3½ litre

Container facet
1   Cans
2   Bottles

Type of beer facet
1   Mild
2   Bitter
3   Lager
4   Stout

Illustrative faceted scheme for a real estate agent's records

Here is a further example of a simple faceted classification scheme, which the reader can attempt to compile, as a practical exercise, if desired, before turning to pages 13 to 14 to discover the answer.

A real estate agent, or broker, is computerizing his records and wishes to devise a coding for the various dwellings that he has for sale. There are four pieces of information that are relevant: (1) number of bedrooms; (2) type of accommodation; (3) area; (4) price. The following are typical examples of his advertisements. Analyse these advertisements in order to obtain a list of relevant concepts and from these compile a faceted scheme that will satisfy the requirement.

4 bedroomed semi-detached bungalow. Atwell. £93,000.

3 bedroomed detached house. Denby. £105,000.

1 bedroomed apartment. Crosswood. £32,000.

5 bedroomed detached house. Blanford. £135,000.

3 bedroomed semi-detached house. Denby. £65,000.

2 bedroomed detached bungalow. Atwell. £85,000.

3 bedroomed terraced house. Crosswood. £41,000.

Where the price facet is concerned it is considered sufficient to indicate broad bands, that is, below £40,000, £40,000-60,000, £60,000-80,000, and so on. In the type of accommodation facet, concepts such as 'detached' and 'house' could be considered separately but, for simplicity, at this stage 'detached house' is to be regarded as a single concept.

Terraced houses

Semi-detached houses

Detached house

Bungalow

The terms in the advertisements on the previous page are those used in the United Kingdom and may be defined as follows:

Apartment	A room or set of rooms fitted with housekeeping facilities, usually on one floor, comprising a single residence in a larger building. Also referred to as a flat.

Terraced house	One of a row of houses in a single block. Also referred to as a town house.
Semi-detached house	One of two houses joined to each other by a party wall on one side only.
Detached house	A separate building standing by itself, not sharing a wall with another building.
Bungalow	A one-storied house with a low roof.

The first step is to analyse the advertisements in order to obtain a list of relevant concepts, that is:

> 4 bedroomed
> semi-detached bungalow
> Atwell
> £80,000-100,000
> 3 bedroomed
> detached house
> Denby
> £100,000-120,000
> 1 bedroomed
> apartment
> Crosswood
> up to £40,000
> 5 bedroomed
> Blanford
> over £120,000
> semi-detached house
> £60,000-80,000
> 2 bedroomed
> detached bungalow
> terraced house
> £40,000-60,000

Note that once a concept is listed, it is not repeated when found in another advertisement.

The second step is to group these concepts into facets according to relevant characteristics, which, in this case, are: number of bedrooms; type of accommodation; area; price range. For example, the first concept is '4 bedroomed' and looking down the list other concepts with these same characteristics can be found, for example '3 bedroomed', '1 bedroomed' and so on. When this process is complete, the result would be:

No. of bedrooms	Type of accommodation	Area	Price range
4 bed.	Semi-det. bungalow	Atwell	£80,000-100,000
3 bed.	Detached house	Denby	£100,000-120,000
1 bed.	Apartment	Crosswood	up to £40,000
5 bed.	Semi-det. house	Blanford	over £120,000
2 bed.	Detached bungalow		£60,000-80,000
	Terraced house		£40,000-60,000

In order to make the price range exhaustive, the highest value in the range has been designated 'over £120,000'.

The third step is to add a notation, for example:

No. of bedrooms	Type of accommodation	Area	Price range
1 4 bed.	1 Semi-det. bungalow	1 Atwell	1 £80,000-100,000
2 3 bed.	2 Detached house	2 Denby	2 £100,000-120,000
3 1 bed.	3 Apartment	3 Crosswood	3 up to £40,000
4 5 bed.	4 Semi-det. house	4 Blanford	4 over £120,000
5 2 bed.	5 Detached bungalow		5 £60,000-80,000
	6 Terraced house		6 £40,000-60,000

The fourth and fifth steps involve choosing a citation order and then a schedule order. Supposing that the order shown above is used for both, then the scheme is complete and the original advertisements can be classified, for example:

2 bedroomed detached bungalow. Atwell. £85,000	=	**5511**
1 bedroomed apartment. Crosswood. £32,000	=	**3333**
5 bedroomed detached house. Blanford. £135,000	=	**4244**
3 bedroomed semi-detached house. Denby. £65,000	=	**2425**

This may well be the sort of result that you have obtained. The scheme would certainly work, in this form, in a computerized system. However, when written down, it is somewhat confusing because, as the reader will have observed, the order of concepts within facets is not helpful. This order (often referred to as 'order in array') should be one that is of maximum assistance to the user of the classification. For example, the concepts of capacity in the classification for beer sales are best listed in increasing order of size, as shown on page 8.

There are many examples of possible helpful orders. In 'Mathematics' one might choose an order of increasing complexity, for example:

> Arithmetic
> Algebra
> Calculus

For the subject 'Hand-guns' an evolutionary order might be chosen, for example:

> Matchlock
> Wheel-lock
> Flintlock

Looking at the facets in the scheme for the estate agent, certain helpful orders do suggest themselves. The number of bedrooms facet and the price range facet are best arranged in numerical order. In the type of accommodation facet, one possible order is to begin with the apartment and 'one-floor' accommodation and then progress to 'more-than-one-floor' accommodation, that is, the house. No particular order is immediately apparent for the area facet; an alphabetical order could be used. Revising the scheme in this way would result in the following:

No. of bedrooms	Type of accommodation	Area	Price range
1 1 bed.	1 Apartment	1 Atwell	1 up to £40,000
2 2 bed.	2 Semi-det. bungalow	2 Blanford	2 £40,000-60,000
3 3 bed.	3 Detached bungalow	3 Crosswood	3 £60,000-80,000
4 4 bed.	4 Terraced house	4 Denby	4 £80,000-100,000
5 5 bed.	5 Semi-det. house		5 £100,000-120,000
	6 Detached house		6 over £120,000

Obviously this arrangement is much more helpful to the user and sample classification numbers would now be:

> 4 bedroomed semi-detached bungalow. Atwell. £93,000   =   **4214**
>
> 3 bedroomed detached house. Denby. £105,000   =   **3645**
>
> 1 bedroomed apartment. Crosswood. £32,000   =   **1131**

5 bedroomed detached house. Blanford. £135,000	=	**5626**
3 bedroomed semi-detached house. Denby. £65,000	=	**3543**
2 bedroomed detached bungalow. Atwell. £85,000	=	**2314**
3 bedroomed terraced house. Crosswood. £41,000	=	**3432**

The impact of citation order

If the estate agent wished to apply this classification not only in his computerized information system but also to his manual filing system, the filing order would be:

1131
2314
3432
3543
3645
4214
5626

A careful examination of this arrangement will indicate that the chosen citation order brings together accommodation with the same number of bedrooms but *separates* similar dwellings (for example detached houses), *separates* areas and *separates* similar prices. Is this what the estate agent would require in his manual system? The estate agent is approached and he states that the main priority is to group first by area, then by dwelling, then by number of bedrooms and lastly by price. In order to achieve this, the citation order must be changed to:

Area → Type of accommodation → No. of bedrooms → Price

The schedule order could be left as shown above and the instruction relating to the citation order changed to:

3rd facet → 2nd facet → 1st facet → 4th facet

giving, for example, classification numbers such as:

4 bedroomed semi-detached bungalow. Atwell. £93,000   =   **1244**

3 bedroomed detached house. Denby. £105,000   =   **4635**

1 bedroomed apartment. Crosswood.   £32,000   =   **3111**

5 bedroomed detached house. Blanford. £135,000   =   **2656**

3 bedroomed semi-detached house. Denby. £65,000   =   **4533**

2 bedroomed detached bungalow. Atwell. £85,000   =   **1324**

3 bedroomed terraced house. Crosswood. £41,000   =   **3432**

However, in practice it is more convenient to write down the scheme in the same order as the citation order or, as is the case with some schemes, in the reverse of the citation order. Here is the scheme in the same order:

Area		**Type of accommodation**		**No. of bedrooms**		**Price range**	
1	Atwell	1	Apartment	1	1 bed.	1	up to £40,000
2	Blanford	2	Semi-det. bungalow	2	2 bed.	2	£40,000-60,000
3	Crosswood	3	Detached bungalow	3	3 bed.	3	£60,000-80,000
4	Denby	4	Terraced house	4	4 bed.	4	£80,000-100,000
		5	Semi-det. house	5	5 bed.	5	£100,000-120,000
		6	Detached house			6	over £120,000

Classification numbers would, of course, remain as above, for example:

4 bedroomed semi-detached bungalow. Atwell. £93,000 =   **1244**

and the filing order would be:

> **1244**
> **1324**
> **2656**
> **3111**
> **3432**
> **4533**
> **4635**

As can be seen, this fulfils the estate agent's requirement. The Atwell,

Crosswood and Denby residences have now been brought together and, within each area, similar accommodation will also be collocated.

Filing order before adjustment of the citation order

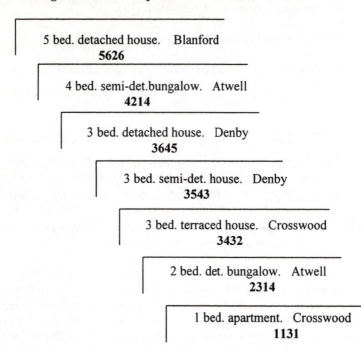

5 bed. detached house.   Blanford
5626

4 bed. semi-det.bungalow.   Atwell
4214

3 bed. detached house.   Denby
3645

3 bed. semi-det. house.   Denby
3543

3 bed. terraced house.   Crosswood
3432

2 bed. det. bungalow.   Atwell
2314

1 bed. apartment.   Crosswood
1131

The decision regarding combination or citation order is clearly very important, for upon this decision will depend which aspects of a subject will be brought together and which will be separated. User needs, therefore, must obviously be taken into account.

Filing order after adjustment of the citation order

Denby.   Detached house . . .
4635

Denby.   Semi-det. House . . .
4533

Crosswood.   Terraced house . . .
3432

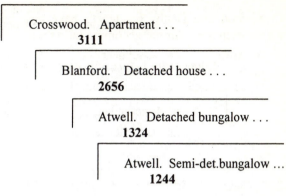

Crosswood.   Apartment . . .
3111

Blanford.   Detached house . . .
2656

Atwell.   Detached bungalow . . .
1324

Atwell.   Semi-det.bungalow . . .
1244

In a computerized information system it would be comparatively easy to search for subjects which did not contain concepts from all facets. The machine could be programmed to find only the concepts required. For example, a 'string' search could be conducted for classification numbers in which the first digit was 2 and the second 1, or for classification numbers in which the first digit was 2, ignoring any further digits. In a manual system, however, it would be necessary to 'build in' the ability to classify such subjects, for example:

　　　　Apartments in Blanford
or　　　Blanford

This could be achieved by using a zero when a concept from a particular facet was not required, thus:

Blanford　　　　　　　　　　　would be classified as　**2000**

Apartments in Blanford　　　　　would be classified as　**2100**

This method would work in a very simple scheme but not in a more complex one. The use of zeros would also have to be carefully monitored in a machine-based system. The computer has a habit of deleting leading zeros from numeric strings. An alternative would be to devise another notational system. For example, a different symbol could be used for each facet in order to distinguish between them. Here is the scheme with upper case letters used for the area facet, lower case letters for the accommodation facet, numeric digits for the number of bedrooms facet and numbers preceded by the letter P for the price facet. (The use of the letter P would then have to be avoided in the area facet.)

Area	Type of accommodation	No. of bedrooms	Price range
A Atwell	a Apartment	1 1 bed.	P1 up to £40,000
B Blanford	b Semi-det. bungalow	2 2 bed.	P2 £40,000-60,000
C Crosswood	c Detached bungalow	3 3 bed.	P3 £60,000-80,000
D Denby	d Terraced house	4 4 bed.	P4 £80,000-100,000
	e Semi-det. house	5 5 bed.	P5 £100,000-120,000
	f Detached house		P6 over £120,000

Whatever the notation chosen, it must reflect and fix the order previously selected for the concepts in each facet (order in array). This can be achieved by using numeric digits or the letters of the alphabet. Note that a mnemonic, or 'memory aid', element has been introduced into certain facets, for example A = Atwell and B = Blanford. (When the notational symbol is the same as the first letter of the concept, this is known as a 'literal' mnemonic.) The reader will already have noticed a mnemonic feature in relation to the 'no. of bedrooms' facet: 1 = 1 bedroomed, 2 = 2 bedroomed, and so on. Sample classification numbers would be:

1 bedroomed apartment. Crosswood. £32,000	=	**Ca1P1**
Apartments in Blanford	=	**Ba**
Blanford	=	**B**

It is also possible to use one type of symbol, for example upper case letters, for all facets and adopt a facet linking device such as the oblique stroke (/), to avoid confusion. Here is the scheme with a notation of this nature:

Area	Type of Accommodation	No. of bedrooms	Price range
AA Atwell	BA Apartment	CA 1 bed.	DA up to £40,000
AB Blanford	BB Semi-det. bungalow	CB 2 bed.	DB £40,000-60,000
AC Crosswood	BC Detached bungalow	CC 3 bed.	DC £60,000-80,000
AD Denby	BD Terraced house	CD 4 bed.	DD £80,000-100,000
	BE Semi-det. house	CE 5 bed.	DE £100,000-120,000
	BF Detached house		DF over £120,000

Sample classification numbers would be:

1 bedroomed apartment. Crosswood. £32,000   = **AC/BA/CA/DA**

Apartments in Blanford   = **AB/BA**

Blanford   = **AB**

A one-letter notation could be used but only if different letters were allocated to each facet, for example A-D for first facet, E to begin the second facet, and so on. If each facet were to begin at A, it would be unclear whether A alone was 'Atwell' or 'Apartment', or '1 bedroomed' or 'up to £40,000'. Similarly, A/A could be 'Atwell apartments' or '1 bedroomed apartments' and so on.

One other requirement needs to be mentioned and that is when two concepts from the same facet are both part of the subject, for example 'Detached houses in Blanford over £80,000 but under £120,000'. A further special connector must be used in order to accomplish classification of such subjects; a plus sign (+) is one possibility, for example:

Detached houses in Blanford over £80,000 but under £120,000

$$= \textbf{AB/BF/DD+DE}$$
$$\text{or} \quad = \textbf{AB/BF/DD +E}$$

This device would also enable 'houses' to be classified, that is, 'terraced houses plus semi-detached houses plus detached houses', for example:

Blanford houses over £120,000 = **AB/BD+E+F/DF**

Now that the reader realizes that concepts from all facets need not necessarily be present in a subject and hence in its related classification number, it will be appreciated that the concepts 'terraced', 'semi-detached' and 'detached' could have been placed in a separate facet. Here is the scheme compiled in this way and presented in the more usual continuous rather than tabular form:

Area
AA   Atwell
AB   Blanford
AC   Crosswood
AD   Denby

Type of accommodation
BA   Apartment

BB   Bungalow
BC   House

Physical situation
CA   Terraced
CB   Semi-detached
CC   Detached

Number of bedrooms
DA   1 bedroomed
DB   2 bedroomed
DC   3 bedroomed
DD   4 bedroomed
DE   5 bedroomed

Price range
EA   up to £40,000
EB   £40,000-60 000
EC   £60,000-80 000
ED   £80,000-100 000
EE   £100,000-120,000
EF   over £120,000

Sample classification numbers would be:

4 bed. semi-detached bungalow. Atwell. £93,000	=	**AA/BB/CB/DD/ED**
1 bed. apartment. Crosswood. £32,000	=	**AC/BA/DA/EA**
Apartments in Blanford	=	**AB/BA**
Blanford	=	**AB**

Notations using primarily capital letters, similar to that shown above, are used, in practice, in schemes such as the *London Classification of Business Studies* (see page 31). In other classification systems a mix of upper case letters for main classes and numeric digits for subdivisions is preferred, as in *Uniclass* (see page 28).

As classification numbers become more complex this can be a problem in a manual system but it matters little in a computer-based environment. The machine can handle very complex notations quite easily. However it should be pointed out that for the coding of manufacturing components and other items in industry a purely numerical and uniform-length notation is sometimes preferred as in the classification of machine bolts described on page 25.

The designer of a scheme must decide, at the concept listing and grouping stage, on the degree to which pre-combination (for example, 'detached house' rather than 'detached' and 'house') is desirable, bearing in mind the aims and objectives of the scheme and the type or types of information system in which it may be used.

The index and introduction

In the above examples it was possible to classify subjects by scanning the classification schedules. However, as the classification scheme develops into a more exhaustive and more complex system, such a scanning process becomes difficult, if not impossible. The scheme will therefore require an alphabetical index to make it more intelligible; that is so that the place in the schedules of a particular concept, and hence its notation, can be ascertained. Extracts from the indexes to faceted schemes are given later (pages 30, 33, 36 and 38). In addition an introduction to the scheme would have to be written. This introduction will explain how the scheme may be used and will provide examples to illustrate this explanation. In a faceted scheme among the more important things to be dealt with are the citation order and the method of notational combination. The introduction, however, should be as brief as possible, subject to clarity and explicitness.

The complete scheme – compilation procedure

Before outlining the compilation procedure for a complete scheme, one final, important point needs to be made. As the reader will probably have noted after examining the illustrative, alphabetic notations on pages 20 and 21, the citation and schedule orders could have a strong influence upon, and must take precedence over, the allocation of notational symbols. Therefore this allocation could, in many instances, more usefully be undertaken *after* decisions relating to those orders have been made. Taking this into account, the full procedure, therefore, would entail the following eight steps:

1   **Analysis**
2   **Grouping**
3   **Order in array**
4   **Citation order**
5   **Schedule order**
6   **Notation**
7   **Index**
8   **Introduction**

As we have seen, all of these would not be essential in every case, for example in a simple scheme for coding entities in a computerized information system.

Where analysis is concerned, appropriate concepts or terms are selected by an examination of the literature of the subject field or fields. It may be sufficient to use sources such as glossaries, dictionaries, encyclopaedias, indexing and abstracting journals and other classification schemes but it might become necessary to look at actual texts when such sources are inadequate or for current terms. The scheme for the estate agent, for example, used terms taken from actual advertisements.

4 Practical Examples of Faceted Classification Schemes

Example 4.1   Classification of machine bolts (Clifton, 1994)

This is a faceted classification of machine bolts for use in a computer-based business system.   It enables each type of bolt to be uniquely identified by a coding.   Such bolts are available in different materials, in different thread sizes, in different head shapes and with different finishes.

Material
  1   stainless steel
  2   brass
  3   steel

Thread size
  1   0 BA
  2   1 BA
  3   2 BA
  and so on

Head shape
  1   round
  2   flat
  3   hexagonal
  4   square

Finish
  1   unfinished
  2   chromium plated
  3   zinc plated
  4   painted

The citation order is the same as the schedule order shown above so that sample classification numbers would be:

Chromium plated brass square head bolts of 2 BA thread   = **2342**

Unfinished steel flat headed bolts of 1 BA thread   = **3221**

A brief introduction would be required in order to explain that the citation order is the same as the schedule order. As this is such a simple scheme, however, no index is required classification can be done by scanning the schedules. It will also be apparent that little attention has been paid to order in array, except in the thread size facet where an ascending order has been used.

Example 4.2   *CI/SfB Construction Indexing Manual* (Ray-Jones,1976 and 1991) and *Uniclass* (Crawford, 1997)

The *CI/SfB* classification has been used extensively for many years throughout the construction industry for organizing office libraries and for the coordination and communication of product information.
    The terms found in the literature of the building industry are grouped into a number of separate facets. There are five broad categories of terms:

Table 0	Physical environment		0 to 9
	eg:	71 Schools	
		94 Sanitary, hygiene facilities	
Table 1	Elements		(--) or (1-) to (9-)
	eg:	(27) Roofs	
		(71) Circulation fittings	
Table 2	Constructions, forms		A to Z
	eg:	S Rigid tile work	
Table 3	Materials		a to z
	eg:	n Rubbers, plastics, etc.	
Table 4	Activities, requirements		(A) to (Z)
	eg:	(Aq) Testing, evaluating	
		(J3) Strength, resistance to deformation	

Classification is achieved, as previously explained, by subject analysis, followed by allocation of the relevant notations to constituent concepts and then by synthesis according to the scheme's instructions for citation order and notational combination. For example, to classify the subject:

Strength of plastic tiles in school roofs

Analysis into concepts:

Strength   Plastic   Tiles   Schools   Roofs

Allocation of notation:

(J3)   n   S   71   (27)

Using the schedule order as the citation order, the classification number is therefore:

71 (27) S n (J3)

This is the citation order to be used when there is no special requirement but *CI/SfB* recognizes that different users may have different priorities.

The notation is very 'mixed'; it includes numeric digits, upper case letters, lower case letters and other symbols. In order to avoid confusion differentiation between facets is achieved either by a change of symbol or by enclosure within brackets. For example, 71 'Schools' is distinguished from 71 'Circulation fittings' by enclosing the latter in parentheses, that is (71).

A subject may contain not only concepts from different facets but also from the same facet, for example 'Sanitary facilities in schools' where 'sanitary facilities' and 'schools' are both from Table 0. A faceted scheme must cater for this eventuality. *CI/SfB* uses a colon to link two concepts from the same facet, for example:

71 : 94

but a colon is not necessary where brackets are already used, so that the subject 'Testing the strength of tiles' would have the classification number:

S (Aq) (J3) or, more correctly, **S (J3) (Aq)**

as *CI/SfB* specifies that the normal citation order within this facet should be: requirement (i.e. strength) – activity (i.e. testing).

CI/SfB enables the classification of very specific subjects but, although such specificity may be required in certain circumstances (for classifying product information for instance), it is recognized that many office libraries will have only a few documents on most subjects and such specificity may not be necessary. In this instance *CI/SfB* recommends a 'basic reference' based mainly on Tables 1 and/or 2 and/or 3 (Ray-Jones, 1991, p.160). As a library expands, *CI/SfB* can provide the extra detail required, as exemplified by the RIBA Library Service.

To facilitate use of the classification an alphabetical subject index is provided. As is usual with a faceted scheme, this index 'contains simple subjects only, and gives the class numbers for single terms such as blocks, bricks, maintenance, retaining walls, and so on, but not for compounds of these (e.g. maintenance of retaining walls)' (Ray-Jones, 1976, p. 177).

In relation to the fact that one must never classify from the index alone (see page 43), the *CI/SfB* index includes the following note on each page: 'Consult the schedules to check the context of items in this index'.

Uniclass (*Unified Classification for the Construction Industry*) was first published in 1997 as the successor to *CI/SfB*. It was developed by consultants from NBS Services (NBS = National Building Specification) and has gradually been gaining acceptance in the industry. *Uniclass* codes have started to appear on trade literature along with the familiar *CI/SfB* codes and a number of institutions are classifying new material by *Uniclass* until natural wastage and careful weeding reduce the original *CI/SfB* stock to manageable proportions for conversion.

Uniclass, as the name implies, is not based solely on *CI/SfB* but also in part on other schemes: *CAWS* (*Common Arrangement of Work Sections for building works*); *CESMM3* (*Civil Engineering Standard Method of Measurement*) and *EPIC* (*Electronic Product Information Co-operation*). It follows the international framework set out in the 1994 ISO Technical Report 14177 *Classification of information in the construction industry*.

The scheme comprises fifteen 'tables', each of which represents a different broad facet of construction information, as compared with five in *CI/SfB*, and the very mixed notation of *CI/SfB* has been greatly simplified. Each facet is allocated a single capital letter (except for classes J and K which have two initial capitals). Concepts within facets are identified by numeric digits. Examples are:

A   Form of information
    eg   A26   Patents
B   Subject disciplines
C   Management
    eg   C42   Marketing, selling
D   Facilities
    eg   D32   Office facilities
               D41   Medical facilities (hospitals)
               D71   Education facilities (Schools)
               D711   Nursery schools

	D712	Primary schools
	D713	Secondary schools
	D714	Sixth form colleges
	D731	Computing facilities, computer rooms
	D94	Sanitary facilities

E   Construction entities
   eg   E2   Tunnels
        E3   Embankments, retaining walls, etc
        E5   Bridges

F   Spaces

G   Elements for buildings
   eg   G24   Roofs
        G331   Floor finishes

H   Elements for civil engineering works

J   Work sections for buildings

K   Work sections for civil engineering works

L   Construction products
   eg   L521   Roof tiles

M   Construction aids

N   Properties and characteristics
   eg   N311   Strength/stability of structures
        N312   Strength of materials, components of structures

P   Materials
   eg   P71   Plastics

Each table can be used as a 'stand-alone' table or terms from different tables can be combined in order to classify complex subjects. Number building is facilitated by the use of three main signs of combination. These are the colon ':', the slash '/', and the plus sign '+'. Those readers who have some knowledge of the *Universal Decimal Classification* (see also page 63) will recognize these signs and they are used in a similar way. The most used sign is the colon since this is the basic mechanism for number building and elements may be combined from the same or from different classes. For example:

Computing facilities in sixth form colleges   =   **D714:D731**

Plastic roof tiles   =   **L521:P71**

The default citation order is the same as the schedule order. However, as with *CI/SfB*, it is 'possible for users to set their own citation order for particular uses, provided that they are not concerned about compatibility with class numbers that another organisation may assign' (Crawford, 1997, p. 15). For example, the subject 'floor finishes in hospitals' would normally be assigned the code D41:G331 but, if a particular organization wishes to give priority to the 'element' rather than to the 'building', then the code G331:D41 could be used.

The '/' is used to indicate a range of *consecutive* elements and the '+' sign is used to indicate a range of *non-consecutive* elements, for example:

Secondary schools and sixth form colleges   =   **D713/D714**

Computing facilities in secondary schools
and sixth form colleges   =   **D713/D714:D731**

Tunnels and bridges   =   **E2+E5**

There are also two specialist signs 'not intended for general use' (*ibid.* p. 13), namely '<' for less than and '>' greater than. These are used to indicate that one concept is a part of another. For example, D32<D71 means 'an office facility which is part of a school'. Here the citation order assumes a critical importance because D71<D32 would mean 'a school which is part of an office facility'.

As in *CI/SfB*, the alphabetical index to *Uniclass* lists concepts only, for example:

Meters L7451
   electricity L74521
   gas L7135
   parking L21531
   water L7118

Ventilation
   natural L7535
   tunnelling M616

A careful examination of these extracts will reveal that the index complements the schedules in that it brings together aspects of a subject that are separated by the scheme. The concept 'Ventilation', for example, can be found in different facets. The index helps to bring together, or 'collocate', the various aspects of the subject. Such an index is known as a 'relative index' and, to use professional jargon, it is said to 'collocate distributed relatives'.

Example 4.3 *London Classification of Business Studies* (2000)

The first edition of this scheme was compiled as a result of the rapid expansion in the field of management education following the establishment of two graduate business schools in the UK (London and Manchester) in 1965. It has established an international reputation and has been used in a number of business libraries and information services throughout the world.

In the scheme the field of business studies is broken down essentially into three main categories:

> Management responsibility within the enterprise

> Environmental studies (ie disciplines such as economics, transport, behavioural science, communication, education, law, political science and science and technology, all of which have some bearing on business and management)

> Basic analytical techniques

Within these broad categories there are a number of main classes such as 'Marketing' (in the 'Management responsibility' category), 'Industries' (in the 'Environment' category) and 'Operational research' (in the 'Techniques' category). Individual concepts are listed within each main class and given a notation consisting of capital letters. The oblique stroke (/) is used as a linking device in order to avoid confusion between facets.

For example, in Class F, Human resource management, FF = 'Pay' and in Class K, Industries, KTC = 'Oil industry'. The recommended citation order is normally the same as the schedule order, that is, alphabetical, therefore:

Pay in the oil industry = **FF/KTC**

Here are some more sample numbers:

Financial management = **EE**

Financial modelling = **EE/TK**
(where TK = Mathematic models)

Online banking   =   **ECB/WE**
(where ECB = Banks and WE = Online operating)

There are two exceptions to the alphabetical citation order noted above. Class A 'Management' is always cited last and Class P 'Law' is always cited first. Therefore:

Management of the oil industry   =   **KTC/AA**
(where AA = Management)

and

Legislation relating to pay   =   **PA/FF**
(where PA = Law or Legislation)

The reasons for these departures from the normal citation order are to keep all law books together and to avoid too much material being classed in management, since much of the literature in business libraries is concerned with this subject (at the time of writing, a search in the London Business School catalogue under 'Management' produced 3,821 'hits'). However, it must be emphasized that the recommended citation order is a *recommendation*, 'there is nothing to stop classifiers using whatever citation order they wish' (Vernon, 1979, p. 10).

A special Auxiliary schedule with a single number (the digit 2) may be added to the classification number for an industry to give the product of that industry. Therefore:

Oil   =   **KTC 2**

Similarly, if KSC is the 'road building industry', then:

Roads   =   **KSC 2**

Other Auxiliary schedules cater for various standard subdivisions such as 'People and occupational roles', 'Place', 'Time' and 'Form'. For example:

Pension schemes for self-employed people   =   **FGB 161**
(where FGB = Pension schemes and 161 = Self-employed people)

Investment management in Singapore   =   **EEN 55362**
(where EEN = Investment management and 55362 = Singapore)

Case studies in strategic management   =   **AD 79**
(where AD = Corporate strategy and 79 = Case studies)

An alphabetical list of subject terms acts not only as an index to the scheme, for example:

. . .

Metrology...................................VW

. . .

Mexico.......................................531

. . .

Microcomputers...........................WBL

. . .

Microeconomics............................JD

. . .

Microelectronics industry............ .KFTE

but also shows the hierarchical relationships that link terms together. This will be discussed more fully in Chapter 13.

Example 4.4   *Colon Classification* (Ranganathan, 1963 and 1987)

This is a general classification of the whole of knowledge for use in libraries. It is a difficult scheme for the beginner to come to terms with but an example of its use is included here because *Colon* was the first scheme to be based entirely on faceted principles. It was devised by S. R. Ranganathan, who was one of the world's foremost classification theorists. Ranganathan introduced a number of new ideas and terms, one of which was the term 'facet'.

Ranganthan taught mathematics at Madras University before becoming the University Librarian of that Institution in 1924. He visited the United Kingdom for observational studies at the School of Librarianship, University College, London, and it was whilst he was there that his analytical mind began to question whether the enumeration of complex subjects was the best basis for a system of classification. He noted, for example, that a subject such as 'Techniques for teaching mathematics in secondary schools' had to be classified by *Dewey* (at that time) either as 'Techniques for teaching mathematics' or as 'Techniques for teaching in secondary schools'. Inspiration came when he visited a London department store and saw for the first time a meccano set. This led him to believe that a classification could be built around a similar methodology; numbers for any subject being constructed by combining the elements listed in the schedules. The first draft of a new classification based upon this idea was completed by 1925. It was called the *Colon Classification* because, initially, he decided to use the colon as a linking device.

In the *Colon Classification* a 'facet formula' for combining concepts is provided for each basic subject or main class and this is followed by lists of the concepts (called by Ranganathan 'isolates' or 'foci') in each facet within that basic subject. Here, for example, is the beginning of Class T Education:

CHAPTER T

EDUCATION

T[P]: [E], [2P], [2P2]

Foci in [P]

1	Pre-secondary
13	Pre-school child
15	Elementary
2	Secondary
25	Intermediate
3	Adult
31	Literate
35	Foreigner
38	Illiterate
4	University

An examination of the concepts (or foci) in [P] and the first part of the 'facet formula' for the class, that is, T[P], will indicate that the subject 'University education' will have the class number T4. The square brackets in the formula are ignored.

Foci in [E] cum [2P]

1	Nomenclature
2	Curriculum
3	Teaching technique

Again an examination of the concepts in [E] and a further look at the formula will indicate that the classification number for 'Teaching methods' is T:3 and for 'Teaching methods in universities' T4:3. The 'cum [2P]' tells us that the concepts in [E] should be linked whenever necessary to those in [2P] and the scheme states:

> Foci in [2P]
> to be got by (SD)

(SD) means subject device and this allows for the use of the classification number for any subject, from the whole of the *Colon* scheme, to be included here in parentheses. For example, 'Mathematics' is Class B and therefore the classification number for the subject 'The teaching of mathematics' would be T:3(B) and for 'The teaching of mathematics in universities' T4:3(B). The comma preceding [2P] is superfluous because of the parentheses.

> Foci in [2P2]
>
> | 1 | Audio-visual |
> |-----|--------------|
> | 13 | Audio |
> | 133 | Gramophone |
> | 136 | Radio |
> | 15 | Visual |

The concepts in the above facet would allow the classification of such subjects as 'The use of visual aids in the teaching of mathematics in universities', which would have the classification number T4:3(B),15.

Citation order in the *Colon classification* always conforms to the one general formula, the PMEST formula, which stands for: Personality (relating to the most important facet which establishes the character of a subject) – Matter (relating to materials) – Energy (relating to processes, activities or operations) – Space (relating to geographical areas) – Time (relating to time periods). This does not mean that the maximum number of facets is five, which would be insufficient for many subjects and multiple 'personality' or other types of facet may be required. In the above Education class formula, for instance, [2P] stands for a 'second round' of the personality facet and [2P2] stands for a second, subsidiary level, of this second round of personality facet. 'Matter' is not in fact present in the Education class.

'Space' and 'Time' may be obtained from special tables that are generally applicable. In these tables 56 is 'Great Britain' and N8 is the 'nineteen eighties'. The connecting symbol for space is a 'dot', or period, and for time is an inverted comma. Therefore:

The use of visual aids in the teaching of
mathematics in British universities today   =   **T4:3(B),15.56'N8**

At first glance, an entry in the index to the *Colon Classification* seems almost unintelligible, for example:

University   2 [P], 34. T [P], 4

However this simply means that the concept 'University' appears in two main classes: first in Class 2 (Library science), where it is included in the 'Personality' facet with the notation 34; second in Class T (Education), where it is again included in the personality facet but with the notation 4. 'University' is therefore a 'distributed relative' which is collocated in this relative index.

An attempt has been made here to present relatively simple examples for illustration purposes. These are taken from the sixth edition (1963). The later, seventh edition (1987),[1] does not appear to have achieved wide acceptance in India, the one country where the scheme has been used extensively. The *Colon Classification* 'is becoming complex and difficult to use' (Foskett, 2000, p. 78). Unfortunately, 'Ranganathan's own concept of "user-friendliness" . . . does not appear to apply to his own scheme's notation as it has now developed' (*ibid.* p. 73). However, it is the principles upon which *Colon* is based that are important and which have led to many applications not only in librarianship but in other fields such as business systems and computing.

Example 4.5 *Broad System of Ordering (BSO)* (1991)

In more recent years only two attempts have been made to produce a new *general* classification scheme based upon modern indexing and classification theory. One is the revision of the *Bliss Bibliographic Classification* (see page 65) and the other is the *Broad System of Ordering (BSO)*. Prepared by the International Federation for Documentation, with the support of Unesco and under the auspices of UNISIST, it was devised essentially by an FID/BSO panel of three classification experts: E.J. Coates, G.A. Lloyd and D. Simandl. Designed for information interchange, subject terms were included on the basis of 'organisational warrant'; a topic was listed only if there was an information centre, source or service devoted to it. It also had a low level of specificity (as the name suggests). Nonetheless, *BSO*, which has been revised and expanded following major testing, could prove very useful as a classification aid in any information system that covers the whole span of knowledge (see also page 129).

Here are some sample class numbers:

100	Knowledge generally
112	Philosophy
200	Science & Technology
250	Space & Earth sciences
252	Astronomy & Astrophysics
,21	Optical astronomy
,28	Satellite astronomy = Spacecraft astronomy
,40	Astrophysics
,70	Solar system astronomy
,72	Sun = Solar phenomena
450	Psychology
460	Education
535	Sociology
560	Law
580	Economics
740	Transport technology & services

Usually, elements of composite subjects within a particular subject field or 'combination area' are cited in reverse schedule order following instructions contained in the scheme, for example:

Satellite studies of solar phenomena　　　=　　**252,72,28**

Codes for composite subjects with elements from different areas are formed by combining notations using a citation order determined by the relationship between elements and by the insertion of a dash or hyphen between them, for example:

Teaching of psychology	=	**450-460**
Philosophy of education	=	**460-112**
Educational psychology	=	**460-450**
Sociology of education	=	**460-535**
Educational legislation	=	**460-560**
Economics of transport	=	**740-580**

Generally applicable facets for time and place are provided, the former being introduced by –01 and the latter by –02. Sample numbers are:

Education since 1920	=	**460-016**
Education in the New World	=	**460-024**

As is the case with other general classification systems with synthetic features, the index does not list all of the possible subject combinations that *BSO* offers. However, some illustrative examples of combinations given in the schedule captions are included. In general structure it is a chain index (see page 110). Here is a sample extract:

Administrative law 567,40
Adolescents, Biomedical sciences 439,34
Adolescents, Mental health & disorders 439,34,38
Adolescents, Psychology 450,53
Adolescents, Social groups 528,34
Adolescents, Sociology 535,74,34
Adoption, Child welfare 575,32,40
Adornment, Fashions & modes 472,25
Adornment & clothing 472
Adornment & clothing, Customs 533,72
Adornment & jewellery 472,80
Adornment articles & clothing, Manufacture 890,472
Adrenals, Biomedical sciences 435,67
Adult and special education 465
Adult education 465,40
Adult language development 911,21,40
Adults, Social groups 528,35
Adventure literature 915,67
Adverse reactions, Pharmacology, Biomedical sciences 425,50,60
Advertising 158,25
Advertising, Commercial 588,82
Advertising & publicity, Commercial 588,80

Note

1   In the latest 7th edition the punctuation marks which precede the various facets are:

,	(comma)	= Personality
;	(semi-colon)	= Matter
:	(colon)	= Energy
.	(full stop	= Space
'	(inverted comma)	= Time

As can be seen, these are very similar to those used in the 6th edition. However, in the PMEST facet formulae at the beginning of each main class the use of abbreviations is abandoned and an attempt is made to provide something more meaningful. In the Education class, for instance, the formula is:

> [Education], [Educated and Educators]; [Properties], [Handling and Techniques].
> [Space]' [Time]

Unfortunately, the 7th edition tends to be very confusing to use and, as noted in the text above, it does not seem to have found favour in the one place where *Colon* has been used extensively, namely India.

References

BSO: Broad System of Ordering (1991), prepared by the FID/BSO Panel (Eric Coates, *et al.*), rev. edn.   Machine-readable version (available on disk and on the Internet at www.classbso.demon.co.)   The copyright of *BSO* is now held by SLAIS (School of Library, Archive and Information Studies), University College London; and the responsibility for its future management now lies with this institution.

Clifton, H.O. and Sutcliffe, A.G. (1994), *Business Information Systems*, 5th edn, Prentice Hall, London; New York.

Crawford, Marshall, Cann, John and O'Leary, Ruth (eds) (1997), *Uniclass: Unified Classification for the Construction Industry*, RIBA, London.

Foskett, A.C. (2000), 'The future of faceted classification', in Rita Marcella and Arthur Maltby (eds), *The Future of Classification*, Gower, Aldershot, Hants; Burlington, VT, pp. 69-80.

London Business School Library (2000), *London Classification of Business Studies*, The Library, 2 v.   This is a new version of the scheme first devised in 1970 by K.D.C. Vernon and Valerie Lang (see below).

Ranganathan, S.R. (1987), *Colon Classification*, 7th edn, edited by M.A. Gopinath, Sarada Ranganathan Endowment for Library Science, Bangalore.

Ranganathan, S.R. (1963), *Colon Classification*, 6th edn, with annexure, Asia Publishing House, Bombay; London.

Ray-Jones, Alan and Clegg, David (1991), *CI/SfB Construction Indexing Manual*, RIBA, London.   Abridged reprint of 1976 revision.

Vernon, K.D.C. and Lang, Valerie (1979), *The London Classification of Business Studies: a classification and thesaurus for business libraries*, 2nd edn rev., K.G.B. Bakewell and David A. Cotton, Aslib, London.

5 Hierarchical Classification

A 'hierarchy', as used in classification, is a series of classes or groups in successive subordination, for example:

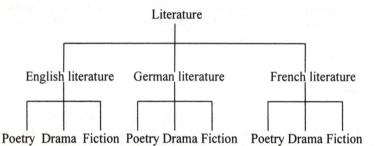

Thus each entity (for example English poetry) falls into a sub-group of a larger group (for example English literature), which in turn forms part of an even larger group (for example Literature).

Such a classification is built up by a process of division, according to certain characteristics. Literature can be divided into sub-classes by the characteristic of language, that is English literature, German literature, French literature. Each of these classes can then be further subdivided by the characteristic of form of literature, that is, English poetry, English drama, English fiction; German poetry, German drama, German fiction; and so on. This is sometimes referred to as a 'top down' approach (as compared with that of a faceted system which utilizes a 'base up' technique).

The tree structure shown above could be presented thus:

This is near to the way in which the classification schedules would be written down or printed.

As the process of division continues the hierarchical classification lists or 'enumerates' (hence 'enumerative' classification) complex subjects, for example 'English poetry', which comprises a language (English) and a literary form (poetry). This may be contrasted with the faceted approach, which would list 'English' and 'poetry' as separate concepts but not as a complete subject.

In a properly designed hierarchical classification each subject should have only one place where it fits into the system.

Order in array

In a hierarchical scheme the order of subjects at a particular level of division is important. This order corresponds to the order of concepts within facets and should be as helpful to the user as possible. For example, in literature, at the language level it would be helpful to place the 'home' language, for example English, first, then related European languages followed by other languages.

Citation order

The citation order in a hierarchical classification is derived from the order in which the characteristics of division are applied. In the literature example, above, the first characteristic of division is language and the second literary form. The citation order is therefore:

Language → Form

but this citation order is 'in-built' to classification numbers for complex subjects listed in the scheme.

Notation

Here is the above scheme with a simple notation consisting of numeric digits added:

1	Literature
11	English literature
111	Poetry
112	Drama
113	Fiction
12	German literature
121	Poetry
122	Drama
123	Fiction
13	French literature
131	Poetry
132	Drama
133	Fiction

This notation may be described as:

Pure	Only one type of symbol is used (the numeric digit).
Expressive	It reflects the structure of the classification; 111 'English poetry' is a division of 11 'English literature', which in turn is a division of 1 'Literature'.
Hospitable	A decimal notation such as this can be added to indefinitely and therefore, in theory, is infinitely expansible.
Mnemonic	'Poetry' is always represented by the digit 1; 'Drama' by the digit 2; 'Fiction' by the digit 3. This type of mnemonic, memory aid is referred to as a 'systematic' mnemonic.

Index

The printed index to an enumerative hierarchical scheme lists complex subjects, for example 'Drama: English literature' (unlike the index to a faceted scheme which lists concepts only). Here is an index to the above schedule:

Drama: English literature	112
Drama: French literature	132
Drama: German literature	122
English literature	11
Fiction: English literature	113

Fiction: French literature	133
Fiction: German literature	123
French literature	13
German literature	12
Literature	1
Poetry: English literature	111
Poetry: French literature	131
Poetry: German literature	121

The index brings together aspects of a subject that are separated in the scheme, for example poetry in various languages. It is therefore a relative index; it collocates distributed relatives.

Process of classification

The process of classification, in an enumerative scheme, is achieved first by consulting the index and then by proceeding to the location pinpointed in the schedules. Although the index lists subjects rather than concepts, one should *never classify from the index alone* as this can lead to error. The relevant schedules *must* be examined in order to find the correct number. To take a simple example, if a book which deals with the work of famous authors such as Shakespeare, Milton and Dickens were to be classified, the index entry for 'Literature' might be referred to and the class number 1 obtained. However after proceeding to 1 in the schedules it will be apparent immediately that 'Literature' is divided by language and the question of whether all the authors dealt with are English language authors must then be considered. Thus the structure of the classification scheme itself acts as an aid in classifying.

Complexity of hierarchical schemes

If the faceted classification of machine bolts shown on page 25 were compiled as a hierarchical scheme, dividing first by material, then by thread size, then by head shape and finally by finish, it would begin to assume the following appearance:

Machine bolts
    Stainless steel machine bolts
        0 BA

          Round
            Unfinished
            Chromium plated
            Zinc plated
            Painted
          Flat
            Unfinished
            Chromium plated
            Zinc plated
            Painted
          Hexagonal
            Unfinished
            Chromium plated
            Zinc plated
            Painted
          Square
            Unfinished
            Chromium plated
            Zinc plated
            Painted
     1 BA
          Round
            Unfinished
            Chromium plated
            Zinc plated
            Painted
          Flat
            Unfinished
            Chromium plated
            Zinc plated
            Painted
          Hexagonal
            Unfinished
            Chromium plated
            Zinc plated
            Painted
          Square
            Unfinished
            Chromium plated
            Zinc plated
            Painted
    2 BA
          Round

Unfinished
Chromium plated
Zinc plated
Painted
Flat
   Unfinished
   Chromium plated
   Zinc plated
   Painted

and so on.

Several things will be immediately apparent:

1   The length of the schedules

    The extract from the scheme shown here has only progressed as far as the subject 'Painted flat 2 BA stainless steel bolts', yet already it is far longer than the faceted scheme.

2   The repetition

    As subjects and not concepts are being listed, constituent concepts such as 'unfinished' have to be repeated every time that they occur in a complex subject.

However, it is still only possible to classify a subject if it is listed. For example, the subject 'Chromium plated stainless steel bolts' (that is, omitting the size) cannot be classified nor can the subject 'Chromium plated bolts'.

Because of the problems (1) and (2) noted above, a hierarchical, enumerative scheme tends to become a compromise and enumeration is not carried to its logical conclusion. Therefore the finished scheme is often very complex in nature and the basic principles of construction are difficult to identify.

6 Practical Examples of Hierarchical Enumerative Classification Schemes

Example 6.1 **Classification for office organization** (Shaw, 1984)

The following are illustrative extracts from a possible enumerative classification for the organization, by subject, of office files.

16	TRAINING
16.1	MATERIALS
16.1.1	Visual aids
16.1.2	Supplies
16.2	COURSES
16.2.1	Clerical
16.2.2	Management
16.2.3	Engineering

The printed index entries to the above schedule would be:

Clerical courses	16.2.1
Courses	16.2
Engineering courses	16.2.3
Management courses	16.2.2
Materials	16.1
Supplies	16.1.2
Training	16
Visual aids	16.1.1

The scheme uses a very simple, expressive, decimal notation and its hierarchical nature is immediately apparent, that is:

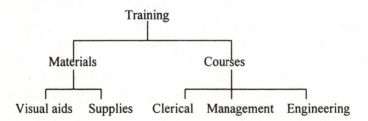

Josephine Shaw, from whose work the above example is taken, suggests that such a system might be suitable for the products, supplies, services and functions of an organization. She cites as an advantage the flexibility which the system offers, in that it is easy to subdivide and add topics, but, in her view, a disadvantage is the fact that an index is essential. She therefore advocates a combination of systems for storing and retrieving information in the office and recommends 'direct filing', that is, alphabetical sequences by name, subject, and so on, where an index is not required.

A hierarchical, enumerative scheme has the further problem that a subject can only be classified if it is enumerated, or listed. To take a simple example from the above scheme, the subject 'Visual aids for clerical courses', cannot be classified. A choice would have to be made between 'Visual aids' (16.1.1) and 'Clerical courses' (16.2.1).

Example 6.2   Guildhall classification for local material (Smith, 1966)

The following extracts are from *Classification for London Literature based upon the Collection in the Guildhall Library*, a scheme for the classification of local materials, that is, materials relating to a specific area, which was first published in 1926:

20-59   Social life

. . .
40-49   Administration - special subjects

. . .
46   Public health and lighting

. . .
46.9   Lighting
46.91   Oil lighting
46.92   Gas lighting
46.93   Electric lighting

The main classes have a two-digit notation, with subdivisions extending to a further two, and sometimes three digits after the decimal point.

The above example illustrates the progressive process of division in an enumerative scheme. However, even in a simple scheme, this process, and especially the consistent application of a particular characteristic of division at one point, is not easy, as the following schedule illustrates:

40   Statistics. Yearbooks
41   Social welfare
42   Crimes. Police
43   Prisons
44   Laws. Courts
45   Markets
47   Medicine. Hospitals
46   Public health and lighting
48   Transport. Traffic
49   Education

Example 6.3   *ACM Computing Classification System* (1999)[1]

This scheme is a revision of the classification system used in the periodical *Computing Reviews*, which itself draws heavily on *Taxonomy of Computer Science and Engineering.*

The heart of the classification is a hierarchical tree, 'restricted to three levels in order [it is claimed] that the tree be able to reflect accurately the essential structure of the discipline over an extended period' (*ACM*, Intro., p. 1).

The top level consists of eleven classes identified by capital letters:

A.   General Literature
B.   Hardware
C.   Computer Systems Organisation
D.   Software
E.   Data
F.   Theory of Computation
G.   Mathematics of Computing
H.   Information Systems
I.   Computing Methodologies
J.   Computer Applications
K.   Computing Milieux

The second and third levels make use of a numeric, decimal division, plus a lower case 'm' for 'Miscellaneous'. In H. 'Information systems', for example, we find:

H.0   GENERAL
H.1   MODELS AND PRINCIPLES
   H.1.0   General
   H.1.1   Systems and Information Theory

H.1.2	User/Machine Systems
H.1.m	Miscellaneous
H.2	**DATABASE MANAGEMENT**
H.2.0	General
H.2.1	Logical Design
H.2.2	Physical Design
H.2.3	Languages
H.2.4	Systems
H.2.5	Heterogeneous Databases
H.2.6	Database Machines
H.2.7	Database Administration
H.2.8	Database Applications
H.2.m	Miscellaneous
H.3	**INFORMATION STORAGE AND RETRIEVAL**
H.3.0	General

and so on

In order to provide sufficient detail, there is also a fourth, unnumbered level which consists of alphabetical subject descriptors. Under H.2.1 'Logical Design', for instance:

H.2.1	Logical Design
	Data models
	Normal forms
	Schema and subschema

In addition to these subject descriptors, there are general terms, such as 'Algorithms', 'Design', and 'Documentation', which can apply to any element when relevant. Names of languages of systems may also be used where appropriate, for example: 'Pascal' under D.3.2 'Language Classification'.

Example 6.4   *Dewey Decimal Classification* (Dewey, 1996)

This is a classification that covers the whole of knowledge. It was devised over a hundred years ago for shelf arrangement in libraries. It has since progressed through twenty-one editions.   Its popularity can be gauged by the fact that it is used in over 200,000 libraries in 135 countries and has been translated into over thirty languages.[2] Because it employs a simple, decimal notation, there are ten main classes:

000	Generalities
100	Philosophy & psychology
200	Religion
300	Social sciences
400	Language
500	Natural sciences & mathematics
600	Technology (Applied sciences)
700	The arts Fine and decorative arts
800	Literature & rhetoric
900	Geography & history

Each main class can be divided into 'ten', in practice nine, sub-classes and each sub-class into nine more, and so on. Here, for example, are some parts of the Literature class, which the reader will see equate closely to the scheme shown on page 42, although the notation is different:

800   Literature
. . .

810	American literature in English
811	Poetry
812	Drama
813	Fiction

820	English and Old English (Anglo-Saxon) literatures
821	English poetry
822	English drama
823	English fiction

830	Literatures of Germanic (Teutonic) languages. German literature
831	German poetry
832	German drama
833	German fiction

840	Literatures of Romance languages. French literature
841	French poetry
842	French drama
843	French fiction

With such a notation, each of the nine subdivisions, for example 821, 822, 823 . . . 829, is theoretically co-equal. As very few subjects divide into nine parts naturally, distortion is bound to occur; nevertheless this is an easily understood system and offers hospitality and expansibility. The *Dewey* scheme utilizes a three-figure 'minimum' base, as illustrated above; further division continues after the decimal point, for example:

822.3　English drama of Elizabethan period

where the '3' represents 'Elizabethan period'. A fifth digit may then indicate a particular dramatist within this period, for example:

822.33　Shakespeare

If an item which deals with a work such as 'a criticism of Shakespeare's Macbeth' were classified by the above scheme, then classification is by subject, but if the actual *text* of Macbeth were to be classified, classification in this case would be by *form*, that is literary form. It will be necessary in a general classification to cater for form classes.

In the above example, the hierarchical method of compilation is easily identifiable, that is division by language, then by literary form, then by period; but this is not always so. Here is a further extract from *Dewey*, taken from class 640 'Home economics and family living':

```
   . . .
641.52    Breakfast
641.53    Luncheon, brunch, elevenses, tea, supper, snacks
641.54    Dinner
641.55    Money-saving and timesaving cookery
641.552      Money-saving cookery
641.555      Timesaving cookery
641.56    Cooking for special situations, reasons, ages
641.561      Cooking for one or two persons
641.562      Cooking for persons of specific ages
641.562         Young people
641.5627        Persons in late adulthood
641.56       Cooking for health, appearance, personal reasons
641.5631        Cooking for persons with illnesses
641.5631           Cooking for persons with heart diseases
641.5631           Cooking for persons with diabetes
641.5632        Cooking with specific vitamin and mineral content
641.5634        High-calorie cooking
641.5635        Low-calorie cooking
641.5636        Vegetarian cooking
641.5637        Health-food cooking
641.5638        Carbohydrate, fat, protein cooking
641.564      Cooking for various specific times of year
641.566      Cooking for Christian church limitations
```

and observances
641.567   Cooking for religious limitations and
observances
541.568   Cooking for special occasions. Including
Christmas, birthdays, celebrations, holidays parties

The above extract shows the great detail of the scheme but it is also somewhat confusing and illustrates the problems of enumeration.   A compromise has had to be reached and the hierarchical process of division has not been continued at each step. For example, division by 'Meal' is not further subdivided by 'Special situations' and then by 'Health' etc but division by each of these characteristics is carried out separately. Thus it is impossible to classify the subject 'Cooking dinner for one' or 'Cooking for persons in late adulthood who suffer from heart disease'. A choice has to be made in these instances between 'Cooking for dinner' or 'Cooking for one' and 'Cooking for persons in late adulthood' or 'Cooking for persons with heart disease'.

What is known as 'cross-classification' also occurs. This happens when different characteristics are applied at the one point of division. For example, 'For special situations' is divided by the characteristics of 'number of people' and 'age' at the one step.

The printed index to the *Dewey Decimal Classification* runs to well over 1000 pages. It is a very detailed, often praised index and its relative nature, which was 'devised and lauded by Melvil Dewey' (the scheme's creator), has had a considerable influence on many other indexes.   Here is an illustrative example:

Muscles	573.75
biology	573.75
drawing	
animals	743.6
humans	743.47
human anatomy	611.73
human physiology	612.74
medicine	616.74
pharmacodynamics	615.773
surgery	617.473
see also Musculoskeletal system	

This indicates that various aspects of the subject 'Muscles' can be found in many different places in the schedules and the cross reference tells the user that additional aspects may be found by consulting 'Musculoskeletal system'.

Dewey classification numbers can become quite lengthy and the digits after the decimal point are sometimes split into groups of three for greater convenience and ease of use, for example:

Muscular dystrophy   362.196 748

The latest edition of *Dewey* is also available on CD-ROM as *Dewey for Windows*, an update disk being issued annually. This electronic version has additional index facilities.

Example 6.5 *Library of Congress Classification* (2001)

This classification was constructed at the turn of the century for the US Library of Congress and it reflects knowledge as represented in the books that are held in this great library's stock. Although designed specifically for the Library of Congress, many libraries, primarily large university and research libraries, have adopted it for their own use, not only in America but in other countries including the United Kingdom.

The scheme consists of some twenty main classes, an alphabetical base enabling each of these to be designated by a capital letter:

A	General works
B	Philosophy, Psychology, Religion
C	Auxiliary sciences of history
D	History: General and Old World (Eastern hemisphere)
E-F	History: America (Western hemisphere)
G	Geography
H	Social sciences
J	Political science
K	Law
L	Education
M	Music
N	Fine arts
P	Language and Literature
Q	Science
R	Medicine
S	Agriculture
T	Technology
U	Military science
V	Naval science
Z	Bibliography. Library science

Some main classes are broken down into sections and a second capital letter used for differentiation purposes, for example:

KD   Law of the United Kingdom and Ireland

KF   Law of the United States

A second upper case letter is also used for major sub-classes:

Q   Science
QA   Mathematics
QB   Astronomy
QC   Physics
.   .   .

Arabic numerals are then used to denote further division, these numbers running, as required, from 1-9999. The following extracts are taken from Class T 'Technology'. Classes are published in separate volumes and the printed Class T contains close on 400 pages. This is only one of upwards of thirty volumes in the complete scheme, which gives some indication of its vast size.

Within Class T, Class TH is 'Building construction', and TH 6000 onwards is concerned with 'Building fittings and their installation'. Here is a brief outline of this section of the scheme:

BUILDING FITTINGS AND THEIR INSTALLATION

6010   General works
.   .   .

6100-   PLUMBING AND PIPEFITTING
7000-   HEATING AND VENTILATION
7700-   ILLUMINATION.   LIGHTING
8000-   DECORATION AND DECORATIVE FURNISHINGS
9000-   PROTECTION OF BUILDINGS

Each of these divisions is further subdivided, for example:

PROTECTION OF BUILDINGS

9025   General works
9031-   Against damage from natural causes
9100-   Protection from fire
9700-   Protection from burglary, sabotage, etc.

The above extracts illustrate the hierarchical nature of the scheme but fail to do the scheme justice in that the printed version of Class TH from division 6000 onwards actually takes up twenty-one pages of complex schedules and the principles of construction become hidden in a wealth of enumerative detail. Here, for instance, are the divisions of one very small section, 'Plumbing of the bathroom':

Plumbing of ... bathrooms. Toilet rooms. Lavatories

6485	General works
6486	General special. Specifications, etc.
6487	Systems
	Details. Fixtures
6488	General works
6489	Catalogs of bathroom fixtures
6490	Basins
	Baths
	Cf TH6518.B3 Public baths
6491	General works
6492	Shower baths. Sprays
6493	Tubs
6494	Foot baths
6495	Sitz baths
6496	Bidets
6497	Soil fixtures
6498	Water closets. Toilets
6499	Urinals
6500	Flush tanks and auxiliary valves, etc.

The subject 'Plumbing of a bidet', for example, would have the class number TH 6496. Despite the detail displayed here, the true nature of the Library of Congress scheme is still not fully revealed. Here is a further extract from 'Heating of buildings':

Heating of buildings

7201	Periodicals, societies, etc.
7205	Congresses
7207	Collected works (non-serial)
7209	Dictionaries and encyclopedias
	Directories
7212	General works
7213	Special localities
	History

7215	General works
7216.A-Z	Country divisions, A-Z
	General works
7221	Early to 1860
7222	1860-
7223	Textbooks
7224	Popular works. Juvenile works
7225	Pocketbooks, tables, rules, etc.
7226	General special
7227	Addresses, essays, lectures
7231	Study and teaching
7325	Specifications
7331	Drawings
	Estimates. Measurements. Quantities and costs
7335	General works
7337	Schedules of prices
7338	Superintendence
7339	Inspection
7341	Testing
7355	Catalogs of heaters and fixtures (General)
7391	Special rooms. By name, A-Z
7392	Special classes of building. By name, A-Z
.A6	Apartment houses
.A8	Atomic bomb shelters
.A9	Automobile service stations
.C56	Chemical plants
.C6	Churches
.C65	Commercial buildings
.C7	Creameries
	Dwellings see TH7201-7643
	Factories see TH7392.M6
.F3	Farm buildings
.F6	Foundries
.G37	Garages
.I53	Industrial buildings
.M2	Machine shops
.M6	Mills and factories
.O35	Office buildings
.P33	Packing houses
.P8	Prisons
.P9	Public buildings
.R3	Railroad structures and buildings
.S35	School buildings. University and college buildings

.S65   Sports facilities
.T34   Tall buildings
.T47   Textile factories
.T5   Theaters
       University buildings see TH7392.S35

A number of points of interest are illustrated by the above example. Among these are:

i   The high degree of 'enumeration'. Even forms such as 'Dictionaries' and 'Encyclopedias' are given in the schedules, for example:

     Encyclopaedia of heating of buildings   =   **TH7209**

ii   The use of alphabetical order within a systematic arrangement by means of initial letters followed by Arabic numbers. The numbers are used decimally and are assigned from special tables in a manner that preserves the alphabetical order. In the above schedule alphabetical division is applied to both geographical and subject division, for example:

     History of the heating of buildings in Japan   =   **TH7216.J3**

     Heating of atomic bomb shelters   =   **TH7392.A8**

     The second example above provides a further illustration of the great detail of this scheme.

iii The use of references to indicate where a particular topic should be classed or to indicate related classes, eg:

     University buildings see TH7392.S35

     TH6490   Baths
                Cf TH6518.B3 Public baths

iv   The provision of hospitality by leaving gaps in the notation (see also page 71).

Each class has its own index and the alphabetical authority list *Library of Congress Subject Headings* (see also pages 103 to 104), since many of the headings include the relevant classification numbers, can act to a limited extent as a general index.

Notes

1   Copyright by Association of Computing Machinery, Inc.
2   http://www.bl.uk/services/bsds/nbs

References

ACM Computing Classification System (1999), Association for Computing Machinery. Available on the Internet at http://www.informatik.uni-stuttgart.de/

Dewey, Melvil (1996), *Dewey Decimal Classification and Relative Index*, edition 21, ed. by Joan S. Mitchell, *et al.*, Forest Press, a Division of OCLC Online Computer Library Center, Albany, NY, 4 v.

Library of Congress (various dates), *Classification*, LC, Washington, 41 v. The examples included here have been checked in 2001 against 'The Library of Congress classification web: pilot test', available from the Cataloging Distribution Service of LC at http://classweb.loc.gov.

Shaw, Josephine (1984), *Administration in Business*, 2nd edn, Pitman, London, p. 91.

Smith, Raymond (1966), *Classification for London Literature based upon the Collection in the Guildhall Library*, 3rd edn, The Library Committee, London.   Cited in George A. Carter (1973), *J.L. Hobbs's Local History and the Library*, 2nd rev. edn, Deutsch, London.

7 The Use of Synthesis in a Basically Enumerative Scheme

It is possible to introduce an element of synthesis, or 'number building', into what is essentially a hierarchical enumerative scheme, in several different ways. This helps to reduce the length of the schedules but improves efficiency.

One method is to provide auxiliary tables of terms that may be applicable throughout the schedules. These tables may include, for example:

Common subdivisions, such as those of form of presentation, for example 'Encyclopedia' or 'Serial'.

Geographical tables for specifying 'place', for example 'United States' or 'United Kingdom'.

Period tables for specifying 'time', for example 'Twentieth century'.

Another method is to include instructions within the schedules themselves for dividing one classification number in the same manner as another. All plants, for instance, may suffer from 'injuries', 'diseases' and 'pests'. Instead of enumerating each of these concepts under every individual plant, they can be listed once and instructions given for the division of each plant in the same way.

PRACTICAL EXAMPLES OF SYNTHESIS IN A BASICALLY ENUMERATIVE SCHEME

Example 7.1 *Bibliographic Classification* (Bliss, 1940-53)

The 1940-53 edition of this general classification scheme for library materials by H.E. Bliss is essentially enumerative but a certain amount of synthesis is provided for by 'systematic schedules', some of which may be applied throughout the scheme but others are applicable only in specific classes. Below are shown extracts from two schedules of the former variety:

SCHEDULE 1

NUMERAL DIVISIONS OF ANY CLASS OR SECTION

. . .
1   Reference books (including dictionaries,
     glossaries, encylopedias, indexes, handbooks...
2   Bibliography...
3   History...
4   Biography...

SCHEDULE 2

GEOGRAPHICAL DIVISION

a   America
aa   North America
. . .
d   Europe
ea   Great Britain

'Education', in the *Bibliographic Classification*, is J, and by use of the above schedules:

A history of education in Great Britain   =   **J3ea**

This number has been derived in a very similar way to the way in which classification is achieved in a faceted scheme. The subject is analysed into its constituent concepts and a notation assigned to each:

History   =   3
Education   =   J
Great Britain   =   ea

The instructions for citation order and method of combination given in the scheme must now be followed. Usually classification would be first by subject, then by 'place' and then by 'form' (for example: Education – Great Britain – Encyclopaedia) but when 'form' is 'history', as in this case, 'place' is cited last (that is: Birds – History – England). As different symbols are used, a linking device is not required.

Bliss was a firm believer in brevity of notation. He thought that the economic limit should be three or four letters or digits. Perhaps because of this, he did not emphasize sufficiently what he refers to as 'composite notation', a general method of number building for complex subjects which he admitted might be necessary for specialist classification. He advocated the possible use of a hyphen to link numbers. Using this method, the classification number for the subject, 'The influence of politics upon the history of education in Great Britain', could therefore be:

J3ea-R   where R is 'Politics'.

Example 7.2   *Dewey Decimal Classification* (1996)

Like the *Bibliographic Classification*, the *Dewey* scheme makes use of generally applicable special tables (seven in the twenty first edition) for standard subdivisions, areas, and so on. In addition, in more recent editions, there is a great deal of provision for synthesis, or number-building, in many specific places throughout the scheme. The instructions at 636.8 'Cats', for instance, are:

636.8 Cats

636.800 1 - .808   Standard subdivisions, specific topics in husbandry of cats
Add to base number 636.80 the numbers following 636.0 in 636.001-636.08, e.g. breeding cats 636.8082, cats for specific purposes other than pets 636.8088
Class cats as pets in 636.8

Referring to 636.0, the general number for 'Animal husbandry', it states that 636.003-636.006 are to be used for standard subdivisions. From Standard subdivision Table 1, 03 = 'Encyclopedias'. Therefore, following the instruction above:

An encyclopedia of cats   =   **636.8003**

Also at 636.0, we find:

. . .
636.08   Specific topics in animal husbandry
. . .
636.081   Selection, showing, ownership marks
. . .
636.082   Breeding
. . .

636.084   Feeding

From this it can be ascertained that the classification number for:

Feeding cats   =   **636.8084**

The above number is derived as follows:

Base number for cats   =   636.80

Add numbers following   636.0
Number for feeding   =   636.084

Add '84' to '636.80'   =   636.8084

The example given in the scheme, 'Breeding cats', is obtained in a similar fashion.

References

Bliss, H.E. (1940-53), *A Bibliographic Classification*, H.W. Wilson, New York, 4 v.
Dewey, Melvil (1996), *Dewey Decimal Classification and Relative Index*, edition 21, ed. by Joan S. Mitchell, *et al.*, Forest Press, a Division of OCLC Online Computer Library Center, Albany, NY, 4 v.

8 Synthesis Grafted on to an Enumerative Scheme

There are two major examples of synthesis being grafted on to an enumerative scheme. The first dates back to the turn of the century when the *Universal Decimal Classification* was formulated. This scheme, which has been issued in a number of different languages and has progressed through a number of editions, was based upon the *Dewey Decimal Classification* but signs of combination and abbreviation were introduced to allow for number building. The second scheme is of much more recent origin and is the ongoing revision of the *Bibliographic Classification.*

Example 8.1 *Universal Decimal Classification (UDC)* (1993)

General number building is allowed for by signs of combination (described previously, as adopted by *Uniclass*, on page 29) that is:

+	Aggregation (the sum of the meanings of several *UDC* numbers)
/	Extension (used for consecutive numbers)
:	Relation

Here are some examples of *UDC* classification numbers. They are the same as their counterparts in the *Dewey Decimal Classification* except that the three-figure minimum is abolished, therefore 310 in *Dewey* becomes 31 in *UDC*:

31	Statistics
51	Mathematics
53	Physics
54	Chemistry
63	Agriculture

Applying signs of combination to the above numbers in order to build up numbers for composite subjects would achieve results as illustrated in the following examples:

Mathematics and physics	=	**51+53**
Physics and chemistry	=	**53/54**
Statistics relating to agriculture	=	**63:31**
	or	**31:63**

There is no stipulated citation order in *UDC*, hence the possible alternative for the last number. This provides for great flexibility (see also pages 29, 72 and 77). If necessary a double colon may be used to 'fix' the order of the constituent elements of a compound number, especially when *UDC* is used in a computer-based information system, for example:

Statistics relating to agriculture	=	**63::31**

Unfortunately *UDC* retains a great deal of enumeration and this can result in conflict with the synthetic facilities. For example, a common auxiliary table for 'persons' (Table I (k) - 05) is applicable throughout the main schedules:

-05 Persons

.   .   .

-053   Persons according to age or age groups

.   .   .

.2   Children and infants

.   .   .

.6   Young persons.   Adolescents.   Teenagers

.   .   .

.8   Adults.   Grown ups

.   .   .

.9   Old persons.   Persons in old age

.   .   .

-055   Persons according to sex and kinship

.   .   .

.1   Male persons.   Men
.15   Boys
.2   Female persons.   Women
.25   Girls

The subject 'Life expectancy' is classified at 314.47 and therefore, by applying the above table:

Life expectancy of men	=	**314.47-055.1**
Life expectancy of women	=	**314.47-055.2**

Similarly, the subject 'Hairstyles' is classified at 391.5 and therefore:

Men's hairstyles	=	**391.5-055.1**
Women's hairstyles	=	**391.5-055.2**

However, the table is not used consistently but is sometimes replaced by enumeration, for example:

391	=	Costume Clothing
391.1	=	Male dress Men's costume
391.2	=	Female dress Women's costume

Similarly:

343.91	=	Kinds of criminal
343.914	=	Women as criminals

Note, however, that the number listed, or enumerated, in the schedules is *shorter* than the number that would have been obtained through the use of synthesis, for example:

Women as criminals	=	**343.91-055.2**

Example 8.2   *Bibliographic Classification.* **Revised edition** (Bliss, 1977-)

A new revision of the *Bibliographic Classification* (see also page 59) based upon facet analysis, began to appear in 1977 and is still in progress. Mills (1976) provides an example that illustrates the difference between the two versions. Within Class U 'Arts/Useful arts', UVC in both the original scheme and the revision is 'Clothing industries'.

Here is an extract from the original scheme:

UVC	Clothing industries
UVD	Men's and boy's clothing
UVDN	Men's and boy's neckties, gloves, hats, caps
UVE	Children's clothing [No enumeration]
UVF	Women's and girl's clothing
UVFL	Women's and girl's underwear, lingerie, hosiery, gloves

A systematic schedule (21) does allow some expansion in this class, for example:

UVE, N   Children's clothing – Patents

But many subjects such as 'Children's gloves' are not enumerated and therefore cannot be classified. One would have to choose between 'Children's clothing', 'Men's and boy's neckties, gloves, hats, caps', or 'Women's and girl's underwear, lingerie, hosiery, gloves'. Specificity is lacking and the choice between class numbers is confusing.

In the revision, UVD becomes 'Products' and within this class various facets are catered for:

UVC	Clothing industries
UVD	Products
	By mode of manufacture, eg:
UVD C	Knitwear
	By material, eg:
UVD E	Textile
	By occasion when worn, eg:
UVD KL	Industrial
	By sex, eg:
UVD S	Female
	By age, eg:
UVD V	Child
	By part of body, eg:
	(trunk and arm)
UVE J	Jacket
	(by extremities)
UVF G	Gloves

All divisions of UV that precede a given classification number may be added directly to that class number but the initial letters common to all of the numbers concerned are dropped. Therefore it is quite easy to classify 'Children's gloves', the class number UVD V 'Child' being added to the classmark UVF G 'Gloves', but without repeating the UV, giving:

Children's gloves   =   **UVF GDV**

The notation of the revision is partly expressive (see pages 42 and 72) and partly ordinal (see page 79). There are also some mnemonic features, for example, J = Jacket, G = Gloves (see also pages 20 and 42). A space is inserted after every three letters for clarity and as an aid to understanding.

The much greater detail provided by the revision may be illustrated further by another example taken from class Q 'Social welfare' (1977). In both the original scheme and the revision QH is 'Housing' (another mnemonic). However, in the original, subdivision is limited and subjects such as 'Housing for old people' cannot be classified. In the revision among the more numerous divisions of class QH we find:

> QH   HOUSING, ACCOMMODATION, SHELTER
>
> . . .
>
> QHX   (By person in need)
>
> . . .
>
> Add to QHX letters G/R following Q in
> QG/QR – eg: Housing for old persons QHX LV

The class number QHX LV is derived from:

> QHX   Housing by person in need

and

> QLV   Old people

As instructed, only the letters following Q in QLV are added to QLX giving:

> Housing for old people   =   **QHX LV**

The new *Bliss* is an ambitious project 'using and developing the work of the Classification Research Group towards the elusive goal of a completely new general classification scheme' (Rowley, 2000).

References

Bliss, H.E. (1977-), *Bliss Bibliographic Classification,* 2nd edn, Butterworths, London, vols in progress.

Bliss, H.E. (1977-), *Bliss Bibliographic Classification,* 2nd edn, Class Q Social welfare, by J. Mills and V. Broughton, with the assistance of Valerie Lang, Butterworths, London.

Mills, J. (1976), 'Bibliographic classification', in A. Maltby (ed.), *Classification in the 1970s,* pp. 25-50.

Rowley, Jennifer and Farrow, John (2000), *Organizing Knowledge: An Introduction to Managing Access to Information,* 3rd edn, Gower, Aldershot, Hants; Burlington, VT, p. 233.

Universal Decimal Classification (1993), International medium edn, English text, Edition 2, British Standards Institution, Milton Keynes, 2v. (BS 1000M:1993).

9 Advantages and Disadvantages of Faceted and Enumerative Classification

Faceted

A faceted scheme lists concepts only — classification numbers for complex subjects are built up by means of synthesis.

Advantages

Because complex subjects are not listed, such schemes are easier to compile.

The schedules are shorter for the same reason but, despite their brevity, they permit the classification of both very simple and very complex subjects.

New subjects can very often be catered for by the combination of already existing concepts.

Disadvantages

The notation can become long and complex and may be unsuitable for the arrangement of documents on shelves as in a library.

The problem of citation order can cause difficulty.

Enumerative

An enumerative scheme attempts to list all possible subjects, both simple and complex, within the defined subject field or fields.

Advantages

Such schemes have been generally accepted and widely used with considerable success throughout the world for a long period of time.

A fairly short and uncomplicated notation can be used.

'Notationally' it is easier to display the structure of the scheme.

Disadvantages

It is impossible to list every conceivable subject.

There can be a lack of accommodation for even simple subjects.

New subjects cannot be accommodated and regular revision may be required.

In relation to the use of general enumerative schemes in libraries, standardization is facilitated because classification numbers may be included in centralized records. For example, *Dewey Decimal Classification* and *Library of Congress Classification* numbers are included in eye-readable and machine-readable records supplied by the Library of Congress and the British Library. With schemes such as the *Dewey Decimal Classification* there is also the possibility of 'integrity of numbers', that is, the stabilizing of existing numbers, a policy initiated by Dewey.

However, general schemes may be unsuitable for certain purposes. For example, in libraries and information services which specialize in particular subject fields, they are not detailed enough in specific areas. Special classification schemes, restricted by subject, are therefore required. Although these may be enumerative or faceted, the latter is now more common. Special schemes are also useful for the manual filing of office papers and for the coding of entities in computerized systems.

10 More about Notation

A common error is to think that choice of notation is the first step in the compilation of a classification scheme. It should now be apparent that this is not so; the allocation of a notation is one of the final steps.

Notation is, however, a very important feature. 'Poor notation can reduce the value of even the best constructed scheme' (Aitchison, 1982). Some of the qualities which might be looked for are:

Uniqueness

Care should be taken that one concept or subject cannot be mistaken for another. In a machine-based system, for example, it could be disastrous if the coding for a component, say a ball-bearing, were the same as that allocated to a completed product such as a gear box. A distinction must however be made between unique identification of a subject and identification of an actual item. For example, in a library using the *Library of Congress Classification*, the subject 'Use of artificial satellites in telecommunication' might have the number TK5104 but there could well be a great number of books dealing with this subject, all with the same class number. For unique identification of each book something must be added to this number, so that in effect it becomes a class+book number. This addition could consist of letters and digits that could represent author, copy number, volume, and so on. A similar situation exists in a computer-based system where a code might be used as the sole key for identification and location of a data record. If several records have the same classification number then some further coding must be added.

Simplicity

Notation should be easily comprehensible and must have ordinal value as it reflects and 'fixes' chosen orders, therefore:

1		A
2	*or*	B
3		C

not

> $
> &
> *

Confusion should be avoided, for example the use of both the upper case letter 'O' and the digit '0', or the lower case letter 'l' and the digit '1'. It is advantageous if notation is easily memorized, written and spoken.

For classification and coding in industry, 'in order to assist the many functions of manufacture by providing a logical and meaningful system of identification for information, data and components . . . the best type of symbolisation is generally considered to be purely numerical and of uniform length' (McConnell, 1971, p. 1).

Brevity

Notation should be as brief as possible. Note that the longer the base, the shorter the classification numbers. For example, using letters, with a base of 26, it is possible to allocate class numbers no longer than two letters to 676 subjects (that is, 26 x 26). Using numerals, with a base of 10, only 100 subjects (that is, 10 x 10) can be allocated numbers no longer than two digits.

Note also that synthesis does not lend itself to brevity in notation.

Hospitality

Notation should have the ability to accommodate new concepts or subjects as necessary. It should allow for the insertion of both subordinate and coordinate subjects. The former is catered for quite easily by the decimal use of numbers (or the use of letters on the same principle). If 1 represents 'Fiction' and 2 'Poetry' then further expansion is possible in this manner:

1	Fiction
11	Historical fiction
12	Romantic fiction
13	Science fiction
2	Poetry
21	Lyric poetry

The insertion of new coordinate subjects is more difficult but it could be provided for by leaving gaps, for example:

1	Construction
4	Testing
7	Maintenance

but the gaps may not be in appropriate places and therefore could interfere with the required order.

Flexibility

It may be useful to be able to alter citation order according to the needs of a particular set of users. Facet analysis lends itself admirably to variations in preferred citation order (see also pages 29 and 77).

Expressiveness

This means that the notation reflects the structure of the scheme and such a notation may also be known as 'structural' or 'hierarchical', for example:

1	Military ordnance
11	Artillery
111	Field artillery

Although sometimes considered helpful (the user can understand the systematic order more easily and it can be an effective tool in hierarchical computer searching), expressiveness is not essential. It results in longer classification numbers and limits hospitality.

Although the above features may be desirable it is obviously going to be difficult to incorporate them all into a single scheme. It is particularly difficult in a faceted scheme, for synthesis does not lend itself to brevity, simplicity, or expressiveness.

Retroactive notation

One device which is sometimes used in faceted schemes in an attempt to shorten numbers is 'retroactive' notation. 'Retroactive' simply means 'backwards'. In notational terms a change of facet is indicated by a reversal of alphabetic or numeric direction from forwards to backwards. A classification number such as:

ABCD

shows no change of direction and therefore is derived from one facet only.
However the classification number:

CDEBCDABC

shows a change of direction, and therefore a change of facet, between the E and the B, and the D and the A. It could have been written as:

CDE/BCD/ABC

but the '/' is superfluous because of the retroactive nature of the number.

In allocating such a notation, it will be seen that the first letters of the alphabet are used to introduce those facets which are to be cited *last* and not for the primary facets. The letter 'A', having been used once, must not be used again in any earlier facet. Similarly 'B', having been used once, must not be used again. Thus the notational base that is available is progressively reduced. Care must therefore be taken that when the primary facets are reached there are still sufficient notational symbols remaining. It is usual to ensure that an adequate amount of the notational base is reserved for the primary facets before allocating a notation to other facets.

Here is a retroactive notation applied to the estate agent's scheme described on pages 11 to 22.

DE	Atwell	CD	Apartment	BC	1 bed.	AB	up to £40,000
DF	Blanford	CE	Semi-det. bungalow	BD	2 bed.	AC	£40,000-60,000
DG	Crosswood	CF	Det. bungalow	BE	3 bed.	AD	£60,000-80,000
DH	Denby	CG	Terraced house	BF	4 bed.	AE	£80,000-100,000
		CH	Semi-det. house	BG	5 bed.	AF	£100,000-120,000
						AG	over £120,000
		CJ	Det. house				

Sample classification numbers would be:

1 bedroomed apartment. Crosswood. £32,000　　=　**DGCDBCAB**

Apartments in Blanford   =   **DFCD**

PRACTICAL EXAMPLES OF NOTATION

Example 10.1   Uniform length, pure notation with unique identification of individual item – from the *NATO Codification System* (Defence Codification Agency, 1997?)

This is a commodity classification and coding plan used by the member countries of NATO (North Atlantic Treaty Organisation). It is based on the Federal supply classification, part of the Federal Catalog System developed in the United States during the period 1946 to 1952 (Defence Codification Agency, p. 2). It is operated, in the United Kingdom, by the Defence Codification Agency (launched in 1996; previous to that year it was known as the Defence Codification Authority) and it is used by the Armed Services in support of inventory management. It enables a unique stock number to be allocated to each item of supply and 'facilitates the interchange of equipment and stores between NATO forces' (MacConnell, 1971, p. 2).

The NATO number (called a NATO Stock Number or NSN) consists of thirteen digits separated into three basic sections. A sample number would be:

5905 — 99 — 023-4567

The first section of four digits is a Group/class prefix which indicates the type of equipment, commodity or component. The first two digits identify a particular group and the next two digits identify a particular subdivision or class within that group. In this section the classification is hierarchical.

Here are some of the main groups, which are allocated numbers between 10 and 99 (some of these numbers are unassigned which leaves room for expansion):

10	Weapons
14	Guided missiles
23	Motor vehicles, trailers and cycles
39	Materials handling equipment
48	Valves
53	Hardware
59	Electrical and electronic equipment

67	Photographic equipment
68	Chemicals and chemical products
71	Furniture
88	Live animals
91	Fuels, lubricants, oils and waxes

As an example, Group 67, 'Photographic equipment' is further divided hierarchically into sub-groups:

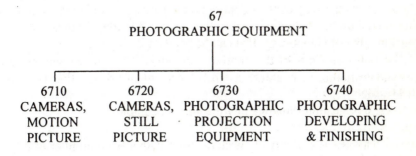

Similarly Group 59 'Electrical and electronic equipment' is further divided into:

5905	Resistors
5910	Capacitors
5915	Filters and networks
etc to:	
5999	Miscellaneous electrical and electronic components

The four digit Group/class prefix 5905 therefore 'identifies the component as a resistor' (*ibid.*).

The second section of the code number is a two digit code to identify the country which originated the equipment or commodity, for example 00 = USA. In the sample number, 99 = Great Britain.

The third section of the code number is the item identification number that contains seven digits, split by a hyphen after the third digit for ease of reading. These digits give uniqueness to the complete NATO number. They are allocated at random by the particular country and have no significant meaning.

Thus, the complete number consists of:

	Group/class prefix	Country of origin	Item identification number
eg:			
	5905	99	023-4567

With only two stages of division in the first hierarchical section and because the Group/class prefix is limited to four digits, two for the main group and two for the sub-group, the maximum number of groups and sub-groups that can be accommodated is 100 x 100 = 10,000. However, this relates only to the subject classification; the further subdivision by country of origin and then by random number in the range 0 to 9,999,999 means that the actual number of components that can be handled is almost infinite.

The last nine digits of the number, comprising the country number and the random number, constitute a NATO item identification that is unique world-wide.

Several points are illustrated by the above example:

1   The use of a purely numeric notation with a fixed number of digits.
2   The hospitality that can be provided by leaving some numbers unassigned.
3   The identification of the country of origin.
4   The addition of a unique random numeric identifier that will distinguish, for instance, the particular component in the above example from other resistors.

Example 10.2   Hospitality – from the *Library of Congress Classification*

In the fifth edition of *Class Q: Science* (Library of Congress, 1951) will be found:

QD   CHEMISTRY

ORGANIC CHEMISTRY

241   Periodicals
243   Yearbooks
245   Collected works
248   History
. . .

'Encyclopedias' are not enumerated or listed, and therefore 'An encyclopedia of organic chemistry' cannot be classified. In the sixth edition of *Class Q* (Library of Congress, 1973) however, appears:

246　　　Dictionaries and encyclopedias

This class number has been neatly slotted into the appropriate place in the scheme by making use of the gap left, for hospitality purposes, in the notation between 245 and 248.

'An encyclopedia of organic chemistry' can now be classified, the number being:

QD 246

The notation is 'mixed' comprising upper case letters and digits.

Example 10.3　Flexibility – from the *London Education Classification* (Foskett, 1974)

In this scheme the facets are arranged in an order of increasing concreteness, for example:

Lab　Teaching methods
.　.　.
Mim　Mathematics
.　.　.
Ras　Primary schools

The recommended or preferred citation order is therefore the reverse of this, for example:

Ras Mim Lab　=　Teaching mathematics in primary schools

It is pointed out, however, by Foskett, the compiler, that individual libraries or information services may wish to vary this order: 'One of the greatest advantages of a faceted classification . . . is that . . . the facets can be arranged in any sequence, to suit the particular user' (*ibid.*, p. 9). If it were desired to bring together all items dealing with 'Teaching methods' and to sub-arrange first by subject and then by environment, then the citation order could be altered to conform to the schedule order and the classification number would become:

Lab Mim Ras   =   Teaching mathematics in primary schools

Note the 'pronounceable' notation. This led to some interesting mnemonic classification numbers, for example:

Bux   Documentation
Pil   Sex education
Ror   Choir schools

Unfortunately in the second edition four-letter notations had to be introduced and the pronounceable element was therefore reduced.

Note also that a change of facet is consistently indicated by a change from a lower to an upper case letter. The upper case letter therefore acts as a facet indicator.

Example 10.4   Expressiveness – from *Uniclass* (Crawford, 1997)

P	Materials
P4	Metal
P41	Steel
P413	Alloy steel
P4131	Stainless steel

Note the way in which the structure of the scheme is reflected in the notation.

Example 10.5   Non-expressiveness – from the *British Catalogue of Music Classification* (Coates, 1960)

PW	Keyboard instruments
. . .	
Q	Piano
. . .	
R	Organ
. . .	
RW	String instruments
. . .	
S	Violin

The structure of the scheme is not revealed by the notation. The 'Piano' and the 'Organ' are both 'Keyboard instruments' but it is not clear that Q and R are subordinate to PW. A similar situation exists with the 'Violin' and 'String instruments'.

A purely ordinal notation such as that shown here, in which no attempt is made to be expressive, permits new concepts to be added anywhere in the schedules and is therefore more hospitable.

Example 10.6 Retroactive notation – from the *British Catalogue of Music Classification* (Coates, 1960)

> G Suites
> P Solos
> Q Piano

As the notation can be combined retroactively, the classification number for:

> Suites for solo piano   =   **QPG**

Note the fact that the facet changes each time that the alphabetical direction reverses.

Example 10.7 Retroactive notation – from the *Bliss Bibliographic Classification* – Revised edition (Bliss, 1977-)

The following example from the revised edition of Bliss was provided on page 67:

> Housing for old people   =   **QHX LV**

A further note is given at QLX, namely:

> * If further qualification is needed, use normal retroactive synthesis retaining 'H' for earlier concepts in class QH – eg: Local authority housing for old people QHX LVH L

The latter number is derived from QHX LV and:

> QHL   Local authority

The 'H' in the latter number is retained but the 'Q' dropped giving:

Local authority housing for old people =   **QHX LVH L**

Again note the change of facet each time that the alphabetical order reverses.

Example 10.8   Retroactive notation – from the *Dewey Decimal Classification* (Dewey, 1996)

Perhaps without realizing it, Dewey included a 'flavour' of retroactive notation in his 'History' class:

History of England

. . .

942.05   History of England in the Tudor period

. . .

942.1   History of London

. . .

942.105   History of London in the Tudor period

Note that whenever the notation returns to '0', that is goes backwards to '0', then the characteristic of division changes from 'Place' to 'Time'.

References

Aitchison, Jean (1982), 'Indexing languages, classification schemes and thesauri', in L.J.Anthony (ed), *Handbook of Special Librarianship and Information work*, 5th edn, Aslib, London, pp. 207-61.

Bliss, H.E. (1977-), *Bliss Bibliographic Classification*, 2nd edn, Butterworths, London, vols in progress.

Coates, E.J. (1960), *The British Catalogue of Music Classification*, British National Bibliography, London.

Crawford, Marshall, Cann, John and O'Leary, Ruth (eds) (1997), *Uniclass: Unified Classification for the Construction Industry*, RIBA, London.

Defence Codification Agency [1997?], *Manufacturer's Guide to NATO Codification System*, The Agency, Glasgow.

Dewey, Melvil (1996), *Dewey Decimal Classification and Relative Index*, edition 21, ed. by Joan S. Mitchell, *et al.*, Forest Press, a Division of OCLC Online Computer Library Center, Albany, NY, 4 v.

Foskett, D.J. and Foskett, Joy (1974), *The London Education Classification: A Thesaurus/Classification of British Educational Terms*, 2nd edn, University of

London, Institute of Education Library. The Institute currently uses a mix of the 1st and 2nd editions with ongoing in-house manuscript revision and modification. At the time of writing the latest version of the scheme is being re-keyed. This is an ongoing but, owing to pressure of work, not a continuous activity and only in-house use is envisaged. (See also page 101n.)

Library of Congress (various dates), *Classification*, LC, Washington, 41 v.; *Class Q: Science*, 5th edn, 1951, and 6th edn, 1973.

MacConnell, W. (1971), *Classification and Coding: An Introduction and Review of Classification and Coding Systems*, British Institute of Management, London.

11 More about Schedule and Citation Order

In the estate agent's scheme with a retroactive notation shown on page 73, the facets are shown in the order of combination, but, in practice, it would be necessary and obviously more useful to set it down in the order of the alphabetical notation:

AB up to £40,000	BC 1bed.	CD Apartment	DE Atwell
AC £40,000-£60,000	BD 2 bed.	CE Semi-det.	DF Blanford
		Bungalow	DG Crosswood

etc.

In fact, this is one of those occasions mentioned on page 16 when the schedule order would differ from the citation order. In this instance citation order would be the *reverse* of schedule order, for example:

1 bedroomed apartment. Crosswood. £32,000   =   **DGCDBCAB**

The citation order may be the reverse of the schedule order not only when retroactive notation is used but whenever it is desired to adhere to the commonly accepted principle that 'general' should precede, or file before 'special'.

If, for instance, in a particular scheme 'Bridge' has the class number Al, 'Construction' the class number B1, and the citation order is 'type of structure' followed by 'operation', then the class number for 'Construction' is B1 and the class number for 'Bridge construction' is AlBl. These numbers would file as:

A1B1
B1

This is not a 'general' before 'special' order. A work on civil engineering construction should file before a work on the construction of a specific structure.

What happens if the same citation order is retained but this is made the reverse of the schedule order? In order to do this the notation must be changed so that the first letter in the alphabetical sequence introduces the first facet to be set down in the schedules, that is:

Operation	Type of construction
Al Construction	Bl Bridge

The classification numbers now become Al for 'Construction' and B1A1 for 'Bridge construction'. These would file as:

Al	Construction
B1A1	Bridge construction

and a 'general' before 'special' order has been achieved. This reflects the 'principle of inversion', which states that filing order should be the reverse of citation order.

Remember, however, that it is not essential for citation order and schedule order to differ.

When various types of symbol introduce different facets a filing order for symbols can be laid down so that a 'general' before 'special' sequence will be obtained. For example, if in a classification scheme for 'Literature', B is 'English literature', 2 is 'Drama' and e is 'Essays', and if facets are combined in this order, then sample class numbers would be:

B2	English drama
B2e	Essays on English drama
Be	Essays on English literature

'Essays on English literature' is more 'general' than 'Essays on English drama' and should come first in a filing arrangement. It may be stipulated therefore that lower case letters file before numbers, giving this order:

Be	Essays on English literature
B2	English drama
B2e	Essays on English drama

which is the 'general' before 'special' order that is required.

Facet formulae

On page 35 reference was made to Ranganathan's PMEST formula. Difficulty can be experienced in the understanding of this formula. What precisely is 'Personality', for example? It is 'remarkably elusive when succinct unambiguous definition is demanded' (Maltby, 1975). However, 'Ranganathan was the first classification theorist to develop an explicit and comprehensive theory for citation order. It was based on the notion of 'decreasing concreteness' – 'those concepts most readily received by the mind (most "concrete") should be cited before concepts less readily received' (Bliss, 1977-). Other theorists have subsequently attempted to produce a generalized facet formula that could be applied more easily. Having identified the primary facet, the 'thing', the objective of study, the end product, then this is cited first. The other facets 'are then cited in an order of dependence; e.g., an operation has to be performed on something and the agent of an operation must have an action to be an agent of' (*ibid.*). This standard citation order can be expressed thus:

Things - Kinds - Parts - Materials - Properties - Processes - Operations - Agents

In certain areas this formula appears to work well. A subject such as 'Machinery for the X-ray testing of stainless steel wires on suspension bridges', for instance, could be analysed thus:

Thing (Bridge) - Kind (Suspension) - Part (Wires) - Material (Steel) - Property (Stainless) - Process (X-ray) - Operation (Testing) - Agent (Machinery)

However, as Foskett (1996) points out, how could such a formula be applied to literature, for example?

Regardless of generalized facet formulae, the important thing is to ensure that the citation order in a particular scheme caters for user requirement.

'Place' and 'Time' do not appear in the formula given above. In fact 'Place' and 'Time' are facets common to many subjects and, even in a faceted scheme, they are often given in 'auxiliary' tables preceding or following the main schedules.

The first part of the formula, 'Thing – Kind', implies that it may well be necessary to introduce sub-facets, or 'facets within facets'. As an example, if a classification scheme for 'Food' were being compiled it would be possible to group according to 'source', for example:

Flesh foods	Grown foods	etc
Fish	Fruit	
Meat	Vegetables etc	
Poultry etc		

A sub-facet could obviously be established for 'Meat', for instance, according to the animal from which it was derived, for example:

Meat
> From cattle
> Beef
>
> From pigs
> Bacon
> Ham
> Pork
>
> From sheep
> Lamb
> Mutton

References

Bliss, H.E. (1977-), *Bliss Bibliographic Classification*, 2nd edn, Butterworths, London, J. Mills and Vanda Broughton, 'Introduction and auxiliary schedules', p. 40.

Foskett, A.D. (1996), *The Subject Approach to Information*, 5th edn, Library Association, London, p. 154.

Maltby, Arthur (1975), *Sayers' Manual of Classification for Librarians*, 5th edn, Deutsch, London, p. 61.

12 Other Features of Classification Schemes

The generalia class

In a scheme which attempts to cater for library materials, there must be provision for documents which do not fall into a particular subject area but which are all-pervasive. Examples are encyclopaedias and dictionaries such as *The Columbia Encyclopedia* or the *Oxford English Dictionary*. What is required, therefore, is a 'general works' or 'generalia' class, which will enable such documents to be classified.

The *Dewey Decimal Classification,* for example, uses Class 000 and, within this class, 030 is used for general encyclopedic works. *Everyman's Encyclopaedia,* being an encyclopaedia in English, would be classified as 032, with the '2' representing English.

Care must be taken to distinguish between a general encyclopaedia and a subject encyclopaedia. Where the latter is concerned classification is first by subject and then by form. An 'Encyclopaedia of cats', for example, would be classified by *Dewey* at 636.8003, as indicated on page 61.

A further example of an all-pervasive topic is in fact 'Librarianship', which is concerned with information handling over the whole range of knowledge. *Dewey* also places 'Library and information sciences' in the generalia class at 020. Within this class 025.4 is 'Subject analysis and control' and the subject of this text, 'Classification', would be allocated the number 025.42.

Literary warrant

The 'literary warrant' principle upon which the *Library of Congress Classification* is based, that is, that the classification reflects the subjects of items actually in stock (see page 53), permits the classification of subjects which often cannot be specified adequately in other schemes, for example:

Shakespeare and Anne Hathaway	=	**PR 2906**
Heat, light and sound	=	**QC 220**

Many books have been written about the subject 'Heat, light and sound' but if, for instance, an attempt is made to classify this subject by the *Dewey Decimal Classification,* it is found to be impossible; the only available choices being:

530 Physics in general
534 Sound
535 Light
or
536 Heat

Literary warrant is however catered for in faceted schemes because the concepts included in such schemes are obtained from the literature of the subject. These concepts may then be combined to form the composite subjects of actual documents. The principle may be illustrated using the *Universal Decimal Classification.* The scheme is based upon the *Dewey Decimal Classification* but, as indicated on page 63, the introduction of signs and symbols permits general number building, therefore:

Heat, light and sound = **534/536**

Main class order

One problem that has exercised the minds of classification theorists is that of the order of the so-called 'main classes' in a general scheme.   The *Dewey Decimal Classification,* for instance, is often criticized for the separation of 'Language' (400) from 'Literature' (800) by 'Science' (500), 'Technology' (600) and 'Arts' (700). But what constitutes a 'main' class? The *Dewey Classification* divides the whole of knowledge into ten such classes but is this feasible? It has no realistic logical base but is primarily governed by the nature of the chosen notation.

It is generally recognized that the order *within* classes is more important than main class order. Is a study of the latter of any significance therefore? Maltby (1975) maintains that, among other things, 'it sets the student to study the structure of the field of knowledge itself'.

A full discussion of main class order is outside the scope of this text. However, one point needs to be made and that is that a major criterion is, of course, the need of the user, which must be paramount. If one main class order is of more help to the user than another then that is the one that should be chosen. This perhaps refers not so much to the overall order but to ensuring that the more closely related classes, for example Language and Literature, Science and Technology, or Sociology and History, are placed in close proximity.

Reference

Maltby, Arthur (1975), *Sayers' Manual of Classification for Librarians*, 5th edn, Deutsch, London, p. 59.

13 The Relationship between Classification and Alphabetical Authority Lists of Indexing Terms — the Compilation of Thesauri

The printed book has been a prime information source for some hundreds of years. A book's alphabetical index unlocks its contents and, without it, a specific piece of information may be very difficult to find. Here are some abbreviated extracts from such an index (Pictorial knowledge, 1970):

aeronautics *see* aviation

aviation

. . .
see also aeroplanes; airships; balloons; gliders

transport

. . .
see also aviation; . . .

A close examination of these entries will reveal a hierarchical structure:

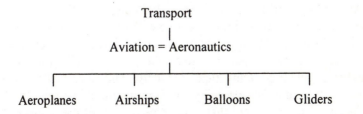

These entries therefore provide a simple example of the use of classification in alphabetical indexing.

Just as an alphabetical index must be provided for a book, so any information system, including a computerized information system, will need to cater for an alphabetical subject approach.

In order to ensure that the selection of indexing terms is consistent, a record or 'authority list' of the terms that have been used will need to be compiled. For example, the entry for 'Aviation', in the authority list, might appear as follows:

Aviation
Use for	Aeronautics
Broader terms:	Transport
Narrower terms:	Aeroplanes; Airships; Balloons; Gliders

This indicates that the lead term 'Aviation' is the preferred term that must be used and that 'Aeronautics' is not to be used. 'Aviation' is subordinate to the broader term 'Transport' and superordinate to the narrower, co-ordinate terms: 'Aeroplanes'; 'Airships'; 'Balloons'; and 'Gliders'.

A further entry in the book index is:

flight

. . .

see also aviation

This additional related term 'flight', which could, of course, be concerned with 'bird flight', would also need to be included in the authority list:

Aviation
Use for	Aeronautics
Broader terms:	Transport
Narrower terms:	Aeroplanes; Airships; Balloons; Gliders
Related terms:	Flight

As a further illustration of how such an authority list might be used, let us take, for example, a library catalogue. In this type of system, when the subject of a document, or some other record, has been ascertained, instead of, or as well as, translating this subject into a classification number, alphabetic indexing terms that succinctly and specifically describe the subject will need to be selected. An examination of a particular document, for instance, might reveal that it is concerned with the subject 'Wages of post office workers'. Using 'natural' language, that is, terms taken directly from the document, the terms that describe the subject are:

Wages
Post office
Workers

If a natural language index is all that is required, then these are the terms that would be used but if consistency is the aim, then an appropriate 'authority list' must be consulted. This may well instruct that 'Post office' is acceptable but that 'Remuneration' is to be preferred to 'Wages', and 'Personnel' is to be preferred to 'Workers'. The terms that must be used are therefore:

Remuneration
Post office
Personnel

The indexing language is being 'controlled' so that the same subjects are consistently indexed under the same terms.

Today, such a structured, controlled vocabulary or indexing language is more often referred to as a 'thesaurus'.

Here is a typical entry from a published thesaurus (Thesaurus, 1997):

Thromboses
   Broader   Cardiovascular Disorders
   Narrower   Cerebral Thromboses
                 Coronary Thromboses
   Related   Embolisms

Clearly, in a similar manner to the illustrative entry for 'Aviation', hierarchical and coordinate relationships or groupings are being established, that is:

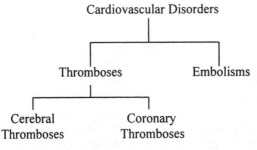

Because the grouping of concepts in this way very obviously embodies a process of classification, can a classification scheme possibly provide a base from which to compile an alphabetically arranged thesaurus? The answer is a very definite 'Yes' and a faceted classification lends itself admirably to this process. The method helps to keep inconsistencies to a minimum and ensures that the thesaurus is grounded upon firm principles.

If, for example, a classification scheme were being compiled for the subject 'People', then the facets would probably include:

People

By age	By sex	By race
Children	Male	European
Adults	Female	Asiatic
etc	etc	etc

The first of these facets will be used as an example to illustrate how a thesaurus can be compiled from such a scheme. A more fully developed facet might appear as follows:

People
    By age
    Babies
    Infants
    Children
    Teenagers
    Adults
        Young adults   *Nb* Sub-facet within Adults
        Middle aged
        Old aged

Having chosen the concepts as shown they should be defined, as certain terms could be interpreted in different ways.

People
    By age
    Babies   0-2 years
    Infants   3-5 years
    Children   6-12 years
    Teenagers   13-17 years
    Adults   over 18 years
        Young adults   18-39 years
        Middle aged   40-59 years
        Old aged   over 60 years

In addition alternative 'non-preferred' forms, if any, of each concept should be indicated at this stage, for example:

People
   Use for persons
     <u>By age</u>

Babies	0-2 years
Infants	3-5 years
Children	6-12 years
Teenagers	13-17 years
Use for Youth	
Adults	over 18 years
Use for Grown up persons	
Young adults	18-39 years
Middle aged	40-59 years
Old aged	over 60 years
Use for Aged	

A thesaurus entry must now be formulated for each concept. The following abbreviations, which have become standard in many thesauri, will be used:

SN	Scope note
UF	Use for
BT	Broader term
NT	Narrower term
RT	Related term

The thesaurus entry for 'Old aged', for example, would be:

Old aged

SN	Over 60 years
UF	Aged
BT	Adults
RT	Young adults
	Middle aged

Note how this entry has been compiled using the already existing hierarchical and coordinate relationships indicated by the classification scheme.

A further entry would have to be made for the alternative non-preferred form of the term 'Old aged', that is:

Aged use Old aged

The reader, if he or she so wishes, may now attempt to produce, in a similar manner, a thesaurus entry for the term 'Adults'. The answer will be found on the next page.

The thesaurus entry for the term 'Adults' would be:

Adults
    SN   Over 18 years
    UF   Grown up persons
    BT   People
    NT   Young adults
          Middle aged
          Old aged
    RT   Babies
          Infants
          Children
          Teenagers

Check this result against your own entry and note that an entry would also be required for the non-preferred term 'Grown up persons', that is:

Grown up persons use Adults

A further point is that, in practice, it is advantageous to alphabetize terms within a particular category of relationship:

Adults
    SN   Over 18 years
    UF   Grown up persons
    BT   People
    NT   Middle aged
          Old aged
          Young adults
    RT   Babies
          Children
          Infants
          Teenagers

Entries for all preferred and non-preferred terms are built up in this way. Completed entries are filed in an alphabetical sequence.

The end result is a systematically developed alphabetically arranged list of terms recommended for use as 'index' terms in retrieval systems, together with an indication of related terms and alternative or synonymous terms.

Such thesauri as those described may be produced as separate entities or they may be published together with the classification scheme from which they were evolved.

Where the classification scheme is not combined with the thesaurus, and is not intended for use in its own right, but is used merely as a basis for thesaurus construction, then compilation is considerably simplified. There is no need to pay attention to such things as order in array (a simple alphabetical order is all that is required), schedule order or citation order.

When the thesaurus is published together with the classification scheme it can then perform a dual function in that it also acts as an index to the scheme. If, for instance, a notation based on upper case letters were added to the 'age' facet, for example:

P	People	
	Use for Persons	
	<u>By age</u>	
PA	Babies	0-2 years
PB	Infants	3 - 5 years
PC	Children	6 - 12 years
PD	Teenagers	13 - 17 years
	Use for Youth	
PE	Adults	over 18 years
	Use for Grown up persons	
PEA	Young adults	18-39 years
PEB	Middle aged	40-59 years
PEC	Old aged	over 60 years
	Use for Aged	

then a typical index/thesaurus entry would be:

Middle aged
 SN 40-59 years   **PEB**
 BT Adults
 RT Old aged
  Young adults

However, the methods of presentation vary and in some schemes it is necessary to consult the classification schedules themselves in order to use the scheme as a full thesaural facility. There follow three examples of classification schemes combined with thesauri, each of which adopts a different method of presentation.

Adults

SN	Over 18 years
UF	Grown up persons
BT	People
NT	Middle aged
	Old aged
	Young adults
RT	Babies
	Children
	Infants
	Teenagers

Aged *use* **Old aged**

Babies

SN	0-2 years
BT	People
RT	Adults
	Children
	Infants
	Teenagers

Children

SN	6-12 years
BT	People
RT	Adults
	Babies
	Infants
	Teenagers

Grown up persons
   use **Adults**

Infants

SN	3-5 years
BT	People
RT	Adults
	Babies
	Children
	Teenagers

Middle aged

SN	40-59 years
BT	Adults
RT	Old aged
	Young adults

Old aged

SN	Over 60 years
UF	Aged
BT	Adults
RT	Middle aged
	Young adults

People

UF	Persons
NT	Adults
	Babies
	Children
	Infants
	Teenagers

Persons *use* **People**

Teenagers

SN	3-17 years
BT	People
RT	Adults
	Babies
	Children
	Infants

Young adults

SN	18-39 years
BT	Adults
RT	Middle aged
	Old aged

Youth *use* **Teenagers**

Sample Thesaurus

Preferred terms are in bold type

PRACTICAL EXAMPLES OF FACETED CLASSIFICATION SCHEMES COMBINED WITH THESAURI

Example 13.1 *London Education Classification* (Foskett, 1974)

The *London Education Classification* (see also page 77) was originally compiled for, and is still used by, the University of London Institute of Education Library.[1] The second edition, influenced by the publication of *Thesaurofacet* (Example 13.2), contains an alphabetical section in thesaural form.

Here is an extract from the classification schedules followed by examples of entries from the index/thesaurus that have been derived from this extract:

Bus	Research in Education
. . .	
But	Research Method . . .
Butj	Data Collection
Butk	Research Technique
Butl	Interview
Butm	Questionnaire
Butn	Survey
Butp	Longitudinal Survey
Butr	Analysis
Buts	Computing
Butt	Statistical Analysis
Butv	Testing Results
Buty	Presentation of results

Sample index/thesaurus entries derived from the above extract

Analysis   Butr
    SN   Examination of research data;
            distinguish from philosophical analysis
    BT   Research Technique
    NT   Computing
            Statistical Analysis
    RT   Interview
            Questionnaire
            Survey
Computing   Buts
    SN   As a research technique
    BT   Analysis
    RT   Statistical Analysis

Research Technique   Butk
  SN   Tactics of research
  BT   Research in Education
  NT   Analysis
        Interview
        Questionnaire
        Survey
  RT   Data Collection
        Presentation of results
        Research Method
        Testing Results

Examine the above entries in the light of the principles explained in the 'People' example. Note how they have been obtained directly from the classification schedules and how they perform the additional function of an alphabetical index to the scheme.   In the case of the *London Education Classification,* concepts listed in the classification schedules are repeated in the thesaurus.   Therefore the alphabetical thesaurus can be used as an entity in its own right, without reference to the schedules.

Example 13.2   *Thesaurofacet* (Aitchison, 1969)

This is a faceted classification and thesaurus for engineering and related subjects, which was developed for use in the English Electric Company (no longer extant as a separate company).   Although now somewhat dated, it is included here because of its importance as the scheme that began the trend to classification-thesaurus integrated systems.

In *Thesaurofacet* related terms indicated by the classification hierarchy are *not* repeated in the index to the scheme. The index includes *additional* related terms only.   In consequence the scheme must be used, whether for classification or alphabetical subject indexing, as an integrated whole.

Here is a brief extract from the schedules:

SV   **Sewage engineering**
SV2   Sewage
SV4   Domestic sewage
SV6   Industrial sewage
SV7   Soil sewage
SV9   Surface water sewage
SVB   Sewers
SVC   Outfall sewers
SVD   Storm sewers

SVE	Manholes
SVG	Sewage pumping
SVH	Syphons (sewage)
SVJ	Sewage treatment
. . .	
SVS	Sewage disposal

and here is the entry for 'Sewage' from the index/thesaurus:

Sewage   **SV2**
UF	Sewerage
RT	Corrosion atmospheres
BT(A)	Wastes

The point to note is that where the term 'Sewage' is concerned, the broader term 'Sewage engineering', the narrower terms 'Domestic sewage', 'Industrial sewage', and so on, and the related terms 'Sewers', 'Sewage pumping' and so on, are indicated in the classification schedules and are therefore not repeated in the index/thesaurus. The thesaurus entry does however contain related terms that are not apparent from the schedules. In this case, for instance, there is the related term 'Corrosion atmospheres' and there is the broader term 'Wastes' (Class SU6) additional to the broader term 'Sewage engineering' revealed by the classification hierarchy. (The 'A' in BT(A) stands for 'Additional'.) Clearly this is an economy device but it does mean that both the schedules and the thesaurus have to be used in order to obtain all the terms related to 'Sewage'.

Thesaurofacet 'had no direct successor' but the *BSI Root Thesaurus* (see page 101) was based upon it (Foskett, 1996).

Example 13.3 *London Classification of Business Studies* (2000)

This classification, already referred to (page 31), also acts as a thesaurus. In earlier versions it was the schedules that performed this function rather than the alphabetical index, which was a conventional location device, but, in the latest revision, it is the alphabetical sequence which indicates hierarchical relationships most clearly.

Here, for example, is a brief extract from the alphabetical sequence:

Retirement.....................................FEFG
   BT   Termination of employment
   NT   Early retirement
         Flexible retirement
         Gradual retirement

Referring to the schedules at FEFG reveals the following:

FEF   **Termination of employment**
FEFB **Resignation**
FEFC **Dismissal**
             UF Discharge
                  Notice
FEFD **Redundancy**
             UF Lay-offs
             RT Severance pay
FEFG **Retirement**
FEFH **Early retirement**
FEFJ **Gradual retirement**
FEFK **Flexible retirement**

In the alphabetical sequence, broader and narrower terms are indicated in the normal thesaural manner. In the classified sequence, the notation and the degree of indentation do not necessarily reveal such relationships. Whilst it seems clear that FEFG 'Retirement' is subordinate to FEF 'Termination of employment', the broader/narrower relationship between 'Retirement' and the particular types of retirement are not explicit.

A related term to 'Redundancy', given at FEFD, which would not be indicated by the classification schedule (as it comes from Class FFPE), is 'Severance pay'. The inclusion of such terms is necessary but they can be difficult to pinpoint as the relationship is not revealed automatically by the scheme.

Abbreviations in thesauri

The abbreviations for Broader terms (BT), Related terms (RT), and so on, being abbreviations of English terms, are language dependent. A more neutral or language-independent system of symbols might be preferred for foreign language or multilingual thesauri. A system has been proposed (British Standards Institution, 1979) that could well form part of a future international standard, that is:

→	precedes the preferred term
=	precedes the non-preferred term
<	precedes the broader term
>	precedes the narrower term
—	precedes the related term

These symbols have been used in the *BSI* (British Standards Institution) *Root Thesaurus* (1985).[2]

Here are the entries for 'Adults' and 'Grown up persons' from the sample thesaurus on page 96 reproduced in this manner:

Adults
    Over 18 years
    =   Grown up persons
    <   People
    >   Middle aged
        Old aged
        Young adults
    —   Babies
        Children
        Infants
        Teenagers

Grown up persons
    →   Adults

Notes

1   The London Institute of Education uses a mix of the 1st and 2nd editions with ongoing in-house manuscript revision and modification. At the time of writing the latest version of the scheme is being re-keyed. This is an ongoing but, owing to pressure of work, not a continuous activity and only in-house use is envisaged. However, 'The rather limited use made of *LEC* outside the Institute's Library belies its importance, since its influence is seen in the categories of the *EUDISED Thesaurus*, Class J Education of *BC2* [the *Bibliographical Classification*, revised edn], in the Educational section of the *UNESCO Thesaurus*, and elsewhere (Aitchison 1982). In fact, the Institute currently uses an adaptation of the *Unesco Thesaurus* for subject retrieval rather than the thesaural part of the *London Education Classification*.

2   The *BSI Root Thesaurus*, based, as noted on page 99, on *Thesaurofacet*, is therefore another example of a scheme that consists of a classified subject display with a complementary alphabetical list. The classified section, which uses facet analysis to assist in the arrangement of the subject fields, gives full information about each term. This information is repeated in the alphabetical list but to one level of hierarchy only.

References

Aitchison, Jean (1982), 'Indexing languages, classification schemes and thesauri', in L.J. Anthony (ed.), *Handbook of Special Librarianship and Information Work*, 5th edn, Aslib, London, pp. 205-261.

Aitchison, Jean, Gomersall, Alan and Ireland, Ralph (1969), *Thesaurofacet: a thesaurus and classification for engineering and related subjects*, 4th edn, English Electric, Leicester.

British Standards Institution (1979), *Guidelines for the Establishment and Development of Monolingual Thesauri*, BSI, Milton Keynes. (BS 5723). Based upon the 'guidelines' previously issued by the International Standards Organisation (ISO 2788).

BSI Root Thesaurus (1988), 3rd edn, British Standards Institution, Milton Keynes.

Foskett, A.C. (1996), *The Subject Approach to Information*, 5th edn, Library Association, London, p. 368.

Foskett, D.J. and Foskett, Joy (1974), *The London Education Classification: a thesaurus/classification of British educational terms*, 2nd edn, University of London, Institute of Education Library.

London Business School Library (2000), *London Classification of Business Studies*, The Library, 2 v. This is a new version of the scheme first devised by K.D.C. Vernon and Valerie Lang in 1970, revised by K.G.B. Bakewell and David Cotton in 1979.

Pictorial Knowledge (1970), International Learning Systems, London, 8 v.

Thesaurus of Psychological Index Terms (1997), 8th edn, edited by Alvin Walker, Jr., American Psychological Association, Washington. The entry cited in the text is taken from the 1974 edition and varies slightly in this latest edition.

Unesco Thesaurus: a structured list of descriptors for indexing and retrieving literature in the fields of education, science, culture, communication and information (1994), New edn, Unesco, Paris. Previous edition compiled by Jean Aitchison, 1977.

Viet, Jean and Slype, Georges van (1984), *EUDISED Multilingual Thesaurus for Information Processing in the Field of Education*, New edn, English version, Mouton, Berlin. At head of title: Council of Europe. Commission of the European Communities.

14 Classification as a Search Tool

Imagine that you are working as a library assistant, or as a bookshop assistant, when a client or customer asks whether you have anything on the 'stegosaurus'. You look on the shelves and, as you might expect, there is nothing specifically on the required subject. Being an efficient assistant, you will check to see if there is anything on 'dinosaurs' or perhaps 'prehistoric animals' or 'prehistoric life', to see if there are any items which contain relevant information. When you carry out a search process in this way, you are making use of classification in that you have identified the superordinate classes to which the required subject belongs.

Use of authority lists and thesauri

The 'stegosaurus' example used above is a simple one. Most people would know that a stegosaurus is a dinosaur. However, one may not always be aware of the context of a particular subject term or of the related terms that might be used as alternative approaches. Alphabetical lists of subject headings, or thesauri, showing related terms, as described in the previous chapter, are useful in this respect and therefore these tools may be used not only for indexing but also for *searching*. An entry such as the following (from the *RCN Library Nursing Thesaurus*, 1998):

> FERTILISATION
> UF   Human fertilisation
> BT   Reproduction
> NT   Assisted conception
> RT   Fertility

indicates that 'Fertilisation' is a term which could have been used as an indexing term and also that the search may be broadened (via 'Reproduction'), narrowed (via 'Assisted conception'), or 'widened', coordinately (via 'Fertility').

The widely used *Library of Congress Subject Headings* (1990)[1] works in a similar fashion, as the following entries illustrate:

Rubber

. . .

UF   Caoutchouc
      Ebonite
      Gum elastic
      India rubber
      Vulcanite
BT   Latex
      Non-timber forest products
RT   Elastomers
      Gutta-percha
NT   Elastic fabrics
      Electric insulators and insulation--Rubber
      Foam rubber
      Guayule rubber
      Vulcanization

. . .

Vulcanite
  USE Rubber

When indexing using this list, whether the document being indexed uses the term 'Vulcanite' or the term 'Rubber' in the constituent text makes no difference. The document *must* be indexed under the term 'Rubber'. In this way, as was explained in the previous chapter, the indexing language is *controlled*. A search for the term 'Vulcanite' would be unproductive but the searcher could, by referring to the list, ascertain that the preferred term is 'Rubber'. In addition, by referring to the term 'Rubber', a range of related terms that could be used in searching will be revealed.

If natural language, where terms are taken directly from the text of a document, is employed, a thesaurus, or an alphabetical subject heading list such as the Library of Congress list, may still assist in the search process.

Imagine that an enquirer is searching a *natural* language system for information on the possible use of parachutes to slow down ocean-going ships. A search is made under 'Parachutes AND Ships' but nothing is found. There is, in fact, a relevant document in the information system entitled 'Putting a halt to super tankers' but the textual content does not include the word 'ship' and, as this is a natural language system, the document has not been retrieved. A check in *Thesaurofacet* (see page 98) indicates that among the possible alternative terms to 'Ships' is the narrower term 'Tankers'. Amending the search to 'Parachutes AND Tankers' will retrieve the document. Without this aid, the searcher would either (a) have assumed, wrongly, that there is nothing relevant in the system, or

(b) have used some other source or even guesswork to come up with possible alternative search terms.

Boolean searching and full text databases

The search for 'Parachutes AND Tankers' utilizes the 'operator' AND to link the two required terms. 'AND' is only one of three operators, the others being 'OR' and 'NOT'. The use of these operators in searching is now very common and widely accepted. AND, OR and NOT are known as *Boolean* operators and this type of searching is referred to as Boolean searching. A search for 'Venice AND Climate' would locate items that had been indexed under both of these terms. A search for 'Venice AND (Climate OR Weather)' would find items which had been indexed under or contained 'Venice' and *either* 'Climate' or 'Weather'. A search for 'Venice AND (Glass NOT Crystal)' would yield those items indexed under 'Venice' and 'Glass' but *not* those indexed under 'Venice' and 'Crystal'.

Today many online information systems contain abstracts or the full text of articles, documents or books. It is now possible to search a complete text, even a large work such as an entire encyclopaedia, for a single word or term, that is full text searching. Because of this, some writers argue that a knowledge of classification is no longer necessary for the information worker. Burton (1997), for instance, maintains, perhaps tongue in cheek, that 'Internet search engines can rapidly find the growing volumes of information created and stored electronically using full text retrieval techniques. These search engines . . . are capable of handling complex search strategies with Boolean operators'. What this statement fails to recognize is that even Boolean searching involves elements of classification. To take a practical example, let us imagine that an enquirer searches for the subject of this book: 'Classification' and the search results in 976 'matches' or 'hits'. This is too great a number of items to browse and many of the items found will be irrelevant as classification can be concerned with a number of different subject areas: 'Biology'; 'Diseases'; 'Plants'; and so on. The enquirer will then add a second term, such as 'Information retrieval' in order to narrow the search to the particular subject area required and thereby reduce the number of items retrieved and increase their relevance.

If we examine what has happened here, this type of searching, although Boolean in that the user is searching for 'Classification AND Information retrieval', can be seen also as a type of classification, in that the user is, in effect, identifying characteristics of a subject in order to bring like items together and separate unlike, the basic principle of classification.

The above Boolean search could be represented diagrammatically thus, the shaded area representing documents that have been indexed under both terms:

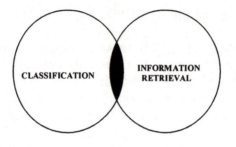

Despite the extensive use of Boolean in online searching, not everyone is convinced that it is the best search methodology. Hildreth (1989), for example, states that 'Much research and experience with Boolean retrieval systems . . . indicates clearly and repeatedly that Boolean search formulation syntax and retrieval techniques are not very effective in search performance and not very usable or efficient search methods for end-users.' 'Determined explorers and the just plain curious need a flexible, rich, contextual subject search and browsing mode which offers plenty of navigation and trail blazing options'. Schneiderman (1997) maintains that 'until recently, computer scientists argued that the best way to search for information on the Web was by using keyword searching . . . But keyword searching often fails miserably'.

There is one word in the first of the above quotes that implies that classification must have a more significant and direct role to play over and above its inherent link with Boolean searching, and that word is 'contextual'. Imagine that a user searches for the term 'Churches' and gets the result:

No items found

Try a more general term

If the user is interested in the church as a physical entity, then, using a similar strategy as in the manual search for 'stegosaurus' already described, he or she might enter the more general, broader term 'Buildings' or perhaps 'Architecture'. Clearly, this type of searching is making use of classification and, where a hierarchical relationship such as this is concerned, the diagrammatic representation would be very different to the Boolean diagram shown above. It would appear thus:

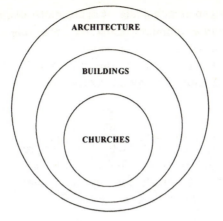

This sort of relationship is therefore not conducive to Boolean type searches but requires some more explicit form of hierarchical classificatory facility.

The distinction between the two kinds of inter-term relationship described here equates with the syntactical (or posteriori) and thesaural (or priori) relationships described in the international standard ISO 2788-1986. The thesaural, or priori, relationship, this standard states, 'adds a second dimension to an indexing language' and 'the effectiveness of a subject index as a means of identifying and retrieving documents' in any system (including 'those systems in which a computer is used to store and manipulate terms or to identify documents associated with terms') 'depends upon a well-constructed indexing language' (International Organization for Standardization, 1986). The use of classification is essential for efficient subject access.

Use of the classification schedule

So far in this chapter we have been concerned with searching under alphabetical terms but it is, of course, also possible to make use of the classification *schedules*. Notation can help solve terminological problems and allow complex subjects to be represented by more simple coding. For example, using the *Dewey Decimal Classification*, a search for 598.2 would find 'Birds', 'Ornithology' and 'Aves'. Also using *Dewey*, a search for 670.427 would equal a search for 'Computer control of factory operations in manufacturing various products' and, using the *British Catalogue of Music Classification*, a search for QPG would equal a search for 'Suites for solo piano'.

When searching a system arranged according to an enumerative classification, the search will usually be made for a classification number that represents the *complete* subject. For example a search for the *Dewey Decimal Classification* number 629.4753 is a search for the subject 'Nuclear propulsion systems for spacecraft'.

When using a faceted scheme, the search *may* be for the complete subject, for example using *Thesaurofacet* for:

RKM/SBH

where RKM is 'Spacecraft' and SBH is 'Nuclear propulsion'; or a 'string' search (that is, a search for a specified string of characters contained within a larger string) could be made for any class number which includes a particular element, for example a search for:

RKM

The idea of searching for a particular element rather than a complete subject can be extended further. In order to understand how this can be done the reader must be aware of the difference between *pre*-coordinate and *post*-coordinate indexing. If the indexer devises an alphabetical subject entry or classification number for the complete subject, for example:

Spacecraft : Nuclear propulsion

or   629.4753

or   RKM/SBH

then this is referred to as pre-coordinate indexing; the significant point being that the concepts, or elements, which together make up the complete subject, are coordinated by the *indexer.*

If the indexer merely indexes the constituent components of the subject, for example:

Spacecraft

or Nuclear propulsion

or   RKM

or   SBH

then this is referred to as post-coordinate indexing. The components of the subject description or class number are left separate and they must be coordinated by the *searcher*. Boolean searching is a post-coordinate method, the terms 'Spacecraft' and 'Nuclear propulsion' could be coordinated, or linked, by the searcher as: 'Spacecraft AND Nuclear propulsion'. Because a faceted classification scheme provides class numbers for separate concepts rather than complete subjects, such a scheme can also be used post-coordinately and searches may be made for subjects such as 'RKM AND SBH'.

Note that a hierarchical enumerative scheme must always be used pre-coordinately but a faceted scheme may be used in either a pre- or post-coordinate manner. When using a faceted scheme post-coordinately no attempt is made to combine class numbers for constituent concepts into a composite number. Citation order and facet linking devices are therefore irrelevant.

Searches can be broadened or narrowed by reducing or increasing the number of elements. For example, using the *London Classification of Business Studies*, a search for 'Safety measures for materials handling in the explosives industry' would be for:

CMG   AND   JZRD   AND   KDQ

where CMG is 'Materials handling', JZRD is 'Safety measures' and KDQ is 'Explosives industry'.

It is then possible to broaden the search by reducing the number of elements. If a search is begun using three elements, as in the above example, each of these could be discarded in turn by searching for:

CMG   AND   JZRD   i.e. 'Safety measures for materials handling'

CMG   AND   KDQ   i.e. 'Materials handling in the explosives industry'

or   JZRD   AND   KDQ   i.e. 'Safety measures in the explosives industry'

Alternatively, the three searches could be combined as:

(CMG AND JZRD)   OR   (CMG AND KDQ)   OR   (JZRD AND KDQ)

The search could be broadened even further by searching for a single element, for example:

KDQ   i.e. 'Explosives industry'

This illustrates the degree of flexibility that can be achieved when searching post-coordinately with a faceted scheme.

Some of the other special facilities introduced to improve alphabetical term searching in computerized systems, can be adapted for use with classification numbers.   An example is the 'truncation' device, that allows searching on word stems; for example a search for 'Comput*' would find 'Computer', 'Computers', 'Computing', 'Computerization' and 'Computerisation'.   This same device can also be used on classification numbers as a means of broadening a search.   Where the previous example of 'Churches' is concerned, in the *Dewey Decimal Classification* this topic would be classified at 726.5.   Truncation would allow the search to be widened progressively.   Searching for:

726.5	would equal a search for	'Churches'
726	"	'Religious buildings'
72	"	'Architecture'

Thus, if a classification scheme is hierarchical and the notation is expressive, the search can obviously be broadened, narrowed or widened in a similar manner to that explained above for a thesaurus.

Chain procedure

The above type of search relates to what Ranganathan referred to as a 'chain', that is, the classification hierarchy for a subject, working through from the general to the more specific.   Such a chain can play a significant part in the search process, not only by the use of classification numbers but also by means of alphabetical entries derived from the classification number by the 'chain procedure' method.   This method can be applied not only to hierarchical classification with expressive notation but also to faceted classification and non-expressive notation.   For example, using the *Universal Decimal Classification*, the classification number for the subject 'Public health aspects of petroleum pollution of sea water' would be:

614.777(26):665.6

This number clearly is not expressive but a hierarchical 'chain' can still be constructed, that is:

6   Technology
61   Medicine
614   Public health
614.7   Pollution
614.777   Water pollution
614.777(26)   Seas
614.777(26):665.6   Oil. Petroleum

Alphabetical subject index entries can be produced from this chain by beginning with the last, or most specific, 'link' and proceeding step by step back through the chain, qualifying where necessary by a more general term or terms to indicate the subject context:

Petroleum: Sea water pollution: Public health	614.777(26):665.6
Oil: Sea water pollution: Public health	614.777(26):665.6
Sea water pollution: Public health	614.777(26)
Water pollution: Public health	614.777
Pollution: Public health	614.7
Public health	614
Medicine	61
Technology	6

The process of qualification would lead to the production of a relative index (see page 30) to the classified arrangement, for example:

Petroleum: Economic geology	553.982
Petroleum: Mining	622.323
Petroleum: Sea water pollution: Public health	614.777(26):665.6

Because of problems relating to terminology and 'missing' or 'false' links, this method is not purely mechanical but semi-mechanical in that some adjustment to the chain, as derived from the classification, may be required. Nevertheless it does provide a means of producing a specific alphabetical entry for a subject, based upon the classification schedule in use, which will indicate the context in which the subject is treated. Entries for related aspects of the same subject can also be pinpointed.

Chain procedure has been applied to a number of information systems, especially in libraries and information services, and it may also be used, either consciously or unconsciously, for book indexing.

The prime example of the successful use of chain is probably the *British National Bibliography (BNB)*. The *BNB* is a weekly list which aims to include all new and forthcoming books published in the British Isles. Works are arranged by the *Dewey Decimal Classification* and name, title and subject indexes to this classified sequence are provided. Chain procedure was used to produce the printed subject index between 1950 and 1970.

PRECIS and COMPASS

When the British Library decided to produce the *BNB* by computerized methods, chain was replaced by PRECIS in 1971. PRECIS was independent of any particular classification scheme but, nevertheless, it had its roots in classification research and was founded on classification principles.

PRECIS is an acronym for PREserved Context Index System and this conveys the intention of allowing a user to enter an alphabetical subject index at any one of the significant terms which together make up a compound subject statement and establish at that point the full context of the subject which contains the selected term. A full statement, a kind of 'precis', is therefore offered to the user under every term in the subject description that the indexer regards as significant enough to be used as an entry word, for example:

> **Aircraft**
>   Engines. Design   629.1343532

Similar entries would be made under 'Engines' and 'Design'.

The above entries illustrate the syntactical side of the system. In addition, the semantic side allows for the automatic production of references to link synonymous or related terms, for example:

> **Motors** *See* **Engines**
>
> **Aeronautics**
>   *See also* **Aircraft**

Authority files of the terms used are built up and maintained thus ensuring that the same subject is consistently indexed under the same form of words whenever it appears.

PRECIS consists essentially of a set of working procedures that produces a linear string of terms summarizing the particular subject. Computer instruction codes are added to this string and the computer will automatically produce appropriate entries. The system is based upon the concept of an *open-ended*, as opposed to a *closed*, vocabulary, which allows for new terms to be admitted at any time.

PRECIS is a sophisticated automated indexing system offering a high degree of versatility but, despite many favourable comments, it was criticized for being over complex. One of the main reasons for this complexity is that it was designed to use the immense power of the computer yet had as its main aim the production of a printed output. Taking the two prime factors of cost-effectiveness and usefulness in an interactive mode into account, a revised system – COMPASS (COMputer Aided Subject System) – was developed. Although simplified, COMPASS entries retained the essential appearance of PRECIS entries.

As noted above, PRECIS was designed essentially for printed output and manual searching. British Library automated systems use a 'holistic' approach reflecting the fact that in such an environment access is made to the whole of the bibliographic record and its data elements. When online, subject information can be retrieved from many parts of the record, not only from standard subject index terms. Where the latter is concerned, in 1995 the British Library reinstated *Library of Congress Subject Headings* (see also pages 103 to 4) to its *BNB* records as the means of controlled language subject access and *Compass* was dropped in 1996.

The Library of Congress still maintains and edits its authority file of subject headings but the file has 'become an increasingly international standard in recent years due to the contribution of new subject heading proposals from libraries across the world'.[2] The printed subject index to the *BNB* also uses Library of Congress headings and *BNB* software arranges the entries producing a lead term followed by the strings in which it occurs, for example:

Heart
Heart. Cytopathology	571.936
Heart. Diseases	616.12
Heart. Diseases. Diet therapy	641.56311
Heart. Surgery	617.412

Systems with multiple search options

The arrangement of the *BNB*, that is a classified sequence with alphabetical indexes, is the sort of arrangement that was used for many years with great success in the catalogues of the majority of British libraries. Such a system is designed to cater for both an alphabetical subject approach or a classified approach.

EXPERT SYSTEMS ⟶ 006.33

006.3   Artificial intelligence
FRANKLIN, Stan
Artificial minds.
Bradford Books, 1995

006.31   Machine learning
KEARNS, Michael J.
Computational complexities
of machine learning.
MIT, 1990.

▶ 006.33   Expert systems
NAYLOR, Chris
Build your own expert system.
2nd edn
Sigma, 1987.

006.3307   Expert systems – Research
HUTTON, Susan M.
Expert systems: teaching and
research.
Loughborough University, 1991.

006.37   Intelligent image processing
BATCHELOR, Bruce
Intelligent image processing
in Prolog.
Springer-Verlag, 1991.

As can be seen from the above diagram, one of the basic features which the traditional, manual, classified catalogue offers is the ability to look in an alphabetical subject index for the classification number for a particular subject and then to go to that number in a classified sequence to find relevant items. Not only is this an efficient way to find all of the items dealing with a specific subject but it also facilitates browsing for coordinate, subordinate and superordinate related subjects.

Computerized catalogues are now the norm, giving the user online access (OPAC = Online Public Access Catalogue). However, in the early stages, many researchers concluded that the online catalogue, despite its numerous virtues, had not improved *subject* access. Some OPACs offered nothing more than a 'keyword from title' facility. Searching under keyword from title obviously requires the title words to reflect the subject clearly. Too often this does not happen; the title *Starting from scratch* is, for example, concerned with teaching methods. Such a title requires 'enrichment' by the addition of appropriate subject terms. Other subject methods tried were little better and, eventually, a number of libraries, including, for instance, those of the University of Warwick and this writer's own Liverpool John Moores University, discovered that the original classified catalogue arrangement could offer a useful methodology for the online catalogue.

Liverpool City Libraries online catalogue also uses such an arrangement. If one searches for the subject 'Classification', some twenty entries are found, including:

CLASSIFICATION : BIOLOGY	574.012
CLASSIFICATION : HUMANITIES	025.460013
CLASSIFICATION : OCCUPATIONS	331.70012
CLASSIFICATION : PLANTS	581.102
CLASSIFICATION : SOCIAL SCIENCES	300.12

Selecting 581.102 would reveal various titles at that number including *An Outline of Plant Classification*, by Sandra Holmes. In addition, the searcher can then scan up and down the classified sequence in a manner similar to that described on the previous page.

This example demonstrates forcibly the value of using a classified approach to improve access. This is not to say that the classified approach should necessarily be *the* approach in an online catalogue. The computer has given us a wonderful, flexible capability that offers search possibilities that were impossible previously and we must make full use of all of these 'added value' facilities. However, to ignore classificatory techniques is to ignore one of the most powerful access tools that we possess.

A computerized online system might provide options via a 'menu', for example:

DO YOU WISH TO SEARCH UNDER
  C CLASS NUMBER
  S SUBJECT TERM
ENTER APPROPRIATE LETTER

The record which describes an item will include both the class number and a field, or fields, containing alphabetical subject terms. Just as in manual systems it may be possible to consult, or browse through, the alphabetical subject index, and other facilities, such as string searching, may be available. If the string search is not confined to a particular field but is extended to include the whole record, then this is referred to as 'free text' searching. A free text search will retrieve a record that contains a search term no matter where in the record the term occurs. It could, for instance, be in a field containing an abstract of an item's subject content. However, free text searching, although extremely useful from the subject search point of view, is outside the scope of a work on classification.

Such facilities can already be found in many online systems but more recent investigation has been concerned with making use of the complete classification scheme for online searching.

For example, the record could contain the class number, the subject terms which are shown alongside the class number in the classification schedules, and the relevant subject index entry from the scheme's index. Using the *Dewey Decimal Classification,* a record for a bibliographic item might contain the following fields:

Class number	623.89
Dewey subject	Nautical engineering and seamanship - Navigation - Selection and determination of course - Including celestial navigation of nautical craft
Dewey index	Navigation - Technology - Seamanship
Author	Taylor
Title	The geometrical seaman

The user would be able to conduct a search in various ways:

1   By class number, for example:
    623.89
2   By pre-coordinate phrases from the alphabetical subject fields, for example:
    Celestial navigation
3   By 'keyword' from the alphabetical subject fields, for example:
    Navigation
    or
    Seamanship

The latter facility would permit 'users to search systematically and receive direction from the system as to fruitful areas of the classification where there are items matching the entered keywords' (Markey, 1986).

In addition the user could browse backwards and forwards through the index to the system, for example:

Navigation - Aids - Maritime transport	387.155
Navigation - Aquatic sports	797.1
Navigation - Law - Maritime transport	341.75676
Navigation - Technology - Seamanship	623.89
Navigators - Biography and work	629.045092

This would assist in the identification of related topics that might also be of use.

Conclusion

Clearly, classification can play an important role in searching, some aspects of which have been described here. There is obviously considerable potential and, where online retrieval systems are concerned, Svenonius (1983) envisaged eight uses of classification:

> In areas of knowledge admitting of natural taxonomies classification can be used to improve recall and precision and to save the time of the user in keying in search terms. In other areas of knowledge, perspective hierarchies can be used to contextualise the meaning of vague search terms, enabling the computer to simulate in part the negotiation of a search request carried out by reference librarians. An important use of traditional classification in online systems is to provide a structure for meaningful browsing. Classification can be used to provide a framework for the representation and retrieval of non-bibliographic information, e.g. statistical data. Automatic classification can be used to collocate citations in ways not possible in manual systems, e.g. by similarity of linguistic features. Finally, classification can be used to achieve compatibility of retrieval languages by serving as a mediating or switching language.

A full explanation of certain possibilities mentioned, that is switching languages and automatic classification, is outside the scope of an elementary introductory text of this nature. However, it may be of benefit to the reader to provide some brief information.

The major objective of a switching language is to enable indexing decisions recorded in one indexing language to be 'translated' into equivalent decisions in another. This is of particular concern when the information systems to be searched are multilingual. Classification schemes such as the *Dewey Decimal Classification* or the *Universal Decimal Classification,* which have been translated into many languages and which make use of an 'international' language, that is, numeric digits, as notational symbols, immediately spring to mind as possible candidates. 'User's search terms entered into the system in one language can be switched through DDC [or UDC] numbers to retrieve documents in several different languages' (*ibid.*). Since this statement was made, machine-readable versions of these schemes have become available, thereby increasing their possible usefulness in a switching role. There is one general classification scheme, namely the *Broad System of Ordering* (see page 36) which has been specifically designed for information exchange and switching, and the *BSI Root Thesaurus* (see page 100) 'has shown that a multilingual thesaurus is feasible — *if* the relationships are shown by symbols rather than letters' (Foskett, 2000).

By removing the human intellectual effort from indexing and allowing the computer to select suitable terms, a form of automatic indexing is obtained. Sparck-Jones (1976) has stated her belief that large files need more sophisticated tools and, since automatic classification has not been conclusively shown to be unhelpful compared with human classification, its longer-term prospects should be of interest to all concerned with information systems. The Internet has acted as a catalyst to revitalize this interest (see pages 129 to 130).

To conclude, the search methodology chosen should be one that is most appropriate for the particular purpose and which is of the greatest assistance to the user. In current online systems subject searching is usually done via alphabetical keywords or subject terms. However, it is now becoming more widely accepted that a greater use of classification in searching could lead to an improvement in search technique and in system efficiency.

Notes

1   The Library of Congress list, which was first published in 1914, is the most comprehensive list of subject headings in existence. From the 13th edition, 1990, it adopted a revised format using the accepted thesaural abbreviations of BT, RT, etc. The list was criticized severely for this move; 'the fact of the matter is that the LCSH list is not a thesaurus, not any more now than it ever was' (Dykstra, 1988). A thesaurus differs from a conventional list such as the LC list in that a listed term need not necessarily be used alone but may be coordinated with other terms. LC headings such as 'Cosmetics for men' or 'Cosmetics containers' or 'Video games and children' would be listed as separate concepts in a true thesaurus. The thesaurus also defines relationships between terms more clearly. Dykstra claims that 'North America has

never bothered to grasp the significance of the research on analytico-synthetic classification that has been undertaken in the rest of the world' (*ibid.*).
2 http://www.bl.uk/services/bsds/nbs/subject.html

References

Burton, Paul (1997), 'The decline and fall of "Cat. and class."', *Catalogue and Index*, 124, p. 9.

Dykstra, Mary (1988), 'LC subject headings disguised as a thesaurus', *Library Journal*, 113 (4), pp. 42-7.

Fosket, A.C. (2000), 'The future of faceted classification', in Rita Marcella and Arthur Maltby (eds), *The Future of Classification*, Gower, Aldershot, Hants; Burlington, VT, pp. 69-80.

Foskett, D.J. and Foskett, Joy (1974), *The London Education Classification: a thesaurus/classification of British educational terms*, 2nd edn, University of London, Institute of Education Library. Ongoing manuscript revisions are produced in-house.

Hildreth, Charles R. (1989), *The Online Catalogue: developments and directions*, Library Association, London, p. 19.

International Organization for Standardization (1986), *Documentation: guidelines for the establishment and development of monolingual thesauri*, 2nd edn, The Organization, Geneva, (ISO 2788), p. 1.

Library of Congress Subject Headings (1995), 18th edn, LC, Washington. Also available on *Classification Plus*, a Windows based CD-ROM. The examples included here have been checked in 2001 against *The Library of Congress classification web: pilot test*, available from the Cataloging Distribution Service of LC at http://classweb.loc.gov

RCN Library Nursing Thesaurus: a thesaurus of terms used in nursing, midwifery, health visiting and related subject areas (1998), 3rd edn, RCN [Royal College of Nursing] Library and Information Services, London.

Svenonius, Elaine (1983), 'Use of classification in online retrieval', *Library Resources and Technical Services*, 27 (1), pp. 76-80.

Schneiderman, R. Anders (1997), 'A non-librarian explains why librarians rule the "Net"', *Information Outlook*, 1 (4), 34-5.

Sparck-Jones, Karen (1976), 'Automatic classification', in Arthur Maltby (ed.), *Classification in the 1970s: a second look*, Bingley, London, pp. 209-225.

15 Classification and the Internet[1]

The two major trends for the accessing of Internet resources were identified by Dodd (1996) as (i) search engines that look for matches on keywords and (ii) the subject-oriented, hierarchical, classification system. 'The explosion of the use of the Internet, particularly via the World Wide Web, has given rise to an interesting phenomenon: the proliferation of semi-professional attempts to give some subject-based access to Internet resources via hierarchical guides ... such as Yahoo.'[2]

Use of classification by search engines

From the beginning Internet search engines recognized the fact that classification can be used for searching the World Wide Web: 'One of Yahoo's prime strengths is the categorising of its contents' (Neely, 1999). An extract from Yahoo's entry screen is reproduced below showing the main categories from which an initial selection may be made.

Arts & Humanities
Literature, Photography...

Business & Economy
B2B, Finance, Shopping, Jobs...

Computers & Internet
Internet, WWW, Software, Games...

Education
College and University, K-12...

Entertainment
Cool Links, Movies, Humor, Music...

Government
Elections, Military, Law, Taxes...

Health
Medicine, Diseases, Drugs, Fitness...

News & Media
Full Coverage, Newspapers, TV...

Recreation & Sports
Sports, Travel, Autos, Outdoors...

Reference
Libraries, Dictionaries, Quotations...

Regional
Countries, Regions, US States...

Science
Animals, Astronomy, Engineering...

Social Science
Archaeology, Economics, Languages...

Society & Culture
People, Environment, Religion...

Each of these main categories is further subdivided into sub-categories. Selecting 'Business & Economy', for instance, will reveal some thirty-five sub-categories, including 'Business Libraries', 'Chats and Forums', 'Electronic Commerce', 'Finance and Investment', 'Labor' and 'Real Estate'. Each sub-category may be subdivided further if desired.

To take a practical example, if a searcher were interested in information on 'Compilers for the programming language C', upon calling up the Yahoo site he or she would find 'Computers and the Internet' included among the listed categories as shown on the screen extract. After selecting this category, 'Programming languages' is among the sub-categories and selecting this will reveal a comprehensive list of languages: 'ABC, Active X, Ada', and so on. 'C and C++' is one of the languages listed and selecting this will reveal a further list that includes 'Compilers', and among the documents listed here is one entitled 'lcc: a retargetable compiler for ANSI C'. An examination of the nature of this search shows that the searcher is being guided through a hierarchical structure (indentation indicating the subordinate topics):

Computers and the Internet
|
   Programming languages
      |
      C and C++
         |
         Compilers

Other search engines provide a similar facility. Using Excite,[3] for instance, if a searcher wishes to find information on 'Careers in the textile industry', selecting the category 'Careers' will reveal a list of sub-categories that includes 'Occupations'. The subdivision of 'Occupations' includes 'Manufacturing' and the list under 'Manufacturing' includes 'Textiles and apparel'.

Excite also has a 'Zoom in' facility, which acts as an aid to help the searcher choose terms which are closer to the required topic. A search for 'Gold', for example, would yield over 3½ million hits! 'Zoom in' would suggest a number of more specific terms that could be tried, including 'Gold prices', 'Gold jewelry' and 'Gold mining'. This is very like the classification-based relative index (see page 111), where an indication is given of the various classes where a particular topic may be found:

    Gold : Finance

Gold : Jewelry
Gold : Mining

One more recent search engines is Google,[4] which has been described as the 'Manchester United' of its sector and as a 'useful search engine. It actually finds what you want quite a lot, rather than millions of links to totally irrelevant information' (Veltman, 2001). Among Google's search facilities is a search by category that it is claimed provides 'a convenient way to refine your search on a particular topic . . . Searching within a category of interest allows you to quickly narrow in on only the most relevant pages to you' (*ibid.*). There are two ways of doing this. One is to work down through the hierarchies in a similar manner to that previously described. For instance, one might choose 'Home' from the top display of categories, then 'Gardens' from the display of sub-categories, then 'Plants' from the categories listed under 'Gardens'. The other way is to search first for a particular topic and then narrow the search by selecting a particular category of interest. For example, if a search is conducted for 'Venus', the result will be a wide range of sites covering subjects such as Venus as a planet, Venus as a Goddess, Venus swimwear, the Venus Dating Agency, Venus Internet Ltd, Radio Venus, and so on. If the hierarchy of categories given against particular sites is examined, for example:

Science > Astronomy

or

Arts > Literature > Myths and Folktales > Myths > Roman

it is comparatively easy to select the category into which your specific requirement falls. Clicking 'Myths' from the last hierarchy above, for example, will retrieve only those sites concerned with Roman mythology.

Dodd (1996) is perhaps right to describe some of these attempts at categorization as 'semi-professional'. Although the hierarchical structures do support subject browsing, the nature of the 'classification' in these search engines does not appear to be as systematic as can be found in the more traditional, established schemes; frequently cross-classification is apparent, and a further disadvantage is that they do not have a notation. Whilst, as has been pointed out earlier in this present work, a notation is not absolutely necessary for a system of classification to work, it can provide added value.

Use of conventional classification schemes

Is it possible, then, to utilize conventional schemes such as the *Dewey Decimal Classification*, the *Library of Congress Classification*, or the *Universal Decimal Classification* for searching the Web? The answer, of course, is a qualified 'Yes', although services which make use of these schemes are usually non-commercial and much more restrictive than the search engines referred to above. Examples of services which use the *Dewey Decimal Classification* are: 'Webrary'[5] and 'The UK Web Library'.[6] The *Library of Congress Classification* is used by 'Cyberstacks'[7] and the 'Scout·Report Archives'[8] uses *Library of Congress Subject Headings*. 'NISS'[9] uses *UDC*. In certain subject areas, the use of special rather than general classification schemes or lists of subject headings may be more appropriate. For example, 'Ariadne',[10] a guide to computer science information on the Web, uses the *ACM Computing Classification System*. 'OMNI',[11] a searchable catalogue of Internet sites covering health and medicine, offers browsing by the NLM (National Library of Medicine) classification scheme, by NLM subject headings and by *MeSH* (Medical Subject Headings).

Webrary is a service provided by the Morton Grove [US] Public Library. The Webrary Links Menu consists of links to what are claimed to be the most useful reference and informational Web sites, organized by *Dewey* class numbers. Selecting one of the ten main classes of *Dewey*:

000-099	Computer science, awards, library science, journalism, museums
100-199	Paranormal phenomena, psychology, ethics
200-299	Religion
. . .	

provides a breakdown of that class, for example for 000:

000- Computers	010- Bibliography	020- Library Science	etc

Upon selecting 020, two of the first relevant sites named are those of the 'American Library Association' and the 'Library of Congress Information System'.

The UK Web Library (WWLib) is provided by the University of Wolverhampton School of Computing and Information Technology. It is produced by spare-time activity and is not supported by the university. The searcher simply enters the classification number for the subject in which he or she is interested. For example if 378 (the *Dewey* number for higher education) were entered, there are 408 entries at that number. Scanning down the subdivisions, the searcher will be shown a series of sites and at 378.42753 is listed the site for this author's own institution, Liverpool John Moores University. One drawback is that an online index to *Dewey* numbers does not appear to be provided.

CyberStacks(sm) is a collection of significant World Wide Web and other Internet resources categorized using the *Library of Congress Classification*. As with Webrary, resources are categorized firstly within a broad classification, for example:

G   Geography, Anthropology and Recreation
H   Social Sciences
J   Political Sciences
. . .

then within narrower sub-classes and finally under a specific classification range and associated subject description. For example, 'T Technology' might be selected from the first list, then 'TL Motor vehicles, Aeronautics and Astronautics' from the sub-classes, and finally 'TL 787-4050 Astronautics' from the specific classification range. A relevant resource listed here is 'NASA Astronaut Biographies'. For each resource, a brief summary is provided and, when necessary, instructions on using the resource. At present CyberStacks(sm) is a prototype demonstration service and is limited to significant WWW and Internet resources in selected fields of science and technology.

The Scout Report Archives is a searchable and browsable database of nearly seven years of the *Scout report*. If, for instance, 'D' is selected from the initial alphabetical array, a list of Library of Congress headings beginning with that letter is displayed. Among these will be found 'Dinosaurs . . . (7)'. This indicates that there are seven subject headings that start with the term 'Dinosaurs'. Selecting this entry will reveal a list of resources entered under appropriate headings: 'Dinosaurs', 'Dinosaurs – Bibliography – Exhibitions', 'Dinosaurs – Cardiovascular system', and so on. Under the last of these headings, for instance, is the resource 'Two on dinoheart'. At the time of writing, 6,541 Scout Report summaries have been assigned subject headings. This service also allows searching and browsing by a subject classification scheme, the *CYRUS Classification*, that was specially developed by the Internet Scout Project.

NISS (National Information Services and Systems), a UK service that provides information for education, uses *UDC* to organize its Directory of Networked Resources. Searchers may browse downwards hierarchically through the classification or, alternatively, browse the 'library shelves' in *UDC* shelfmark order, as illustrated in the following extract from class 3:

34   Law
343 Criminal law
35   Government
352 Local government
353 Regional government
354 Central government
355 Military science. War
36   Social welfare
368 Insurance
37   Education

Selecting a specific classmark will give a list of the resources at that number.

The *ACM Computing Classification System* (see page 48) is used in the Ariadne service and, when a subject is selected, numbers in parentheses denote the total number of entries and the number of quality-checked entries for each class, for example:

D   Software (2604.0/333.0)
. . .
D.3   Programming languages (1000.0/48.0)
. . .

Selecting D.3 will reveal further subdivisions, eg: 'D.3.2 Language Classifications (339.0/21.0)' and selecting this division will reveal a list of annotated resources, for example: 'The Java sourcebook' and 'Python language – NL mirror'.

It should be noted that services such as Webrary, the UK Web Library, the Scout Report Archives, NISS and Ariadne offer other facilities such as searching by keywords. However, as stated above, these services are far less exhaustive than commercial search engines. They are more properly described as search *directories* or *catalogues* rather than search *engines*.

The latter attempt to seek out as many as possible of the Web pages that match a particular search criteria. The former are more selective in that they are limited to a particular directory's database; sites are usually categorized and therefore this type of directory is more likely to utilize hierarchically organized and cross-referenced structures. The difference in coverage can be illustrated by the fact that the 408 'hits' for 'Higher Education' on UK Web Library compares with 17,643 on Yahoo.

Among the search options offered by SOSIG[12] (the SOcial Science Information Gateway) is an online thesaurus (see also page 103). This is a utility that provides the searcher with lists of alternative search terms. The aim is to help increase the accuracy of the search, should the initial attempt retrieve few or no relevant results. The thesaurus contains listings of terms used within the SOSIG Internet catalogue, organised into a hierarchy of relationships. Here, for example, are the terms listed under 'Offences':

Current term: offences

Broader terms:	Narrower terms:	Related terms:
crime	addiction	criminals
	burglary	delinquency
	child abuse	punishment
	civil disturbances	
	driving offences	
	fraud	
	homicide	
	kidnapping	
	perjury	
	rape	
	sexual offences	
	smuggling	
	subversive activities	
	terrorism	
	theft	
	violence	
	war crimes	

Online public access catalogues (OPACs)

As described in the previous chapter, most libraries now have online public access to their catalogues. Many of these catalogues are available on the Internet. Thus is it possible to sit at home and use one's computer to search a great number of systems for citations and availability of required documents. In many instances classification plays a central role in this search process. Some institutions provide merely a version of the in-house system. Other institutions are more innovative. The London Business School, for example, provides 'Concept Space',[13] a visual search tool for business concepts linked to a wide range of information sources. This is a 'point and click' system based upon the *London Classification of Business Studies* (see pages 31 and 99). It is possible to navigate through the system using a 'graphic' view or a 'text' view. Colour coding is used in both views: red = entry term; green = broader term; blue = narrower term; purple = related term. Having found a relevant term in either view, the user can click on the 'Search Resources' link in order to ascertain what material is available.   Here is the 'text' view for the term 'Wages' (minus the colour coding):

Wages

Scope
Excluding fringe benefits, financial and otherwise

Broader
Human resource management

Narrower
Allowances
Deductions from pay
Equal pay
Fees
Guaranteed wage
Incremental payment systems
Job evaluation
Low pay
Pay differentials
Pay incentives
Salary administration

Related
Prices and incomes policy
Wages policy
Wages theory

Synonyms
Preferred term: Pay
Compensation
Payment systems
Remuneration
Salaries
Salary structure

Class mark
FF

Classification of electronic documents

MacLennan (2000) considers that if Internet resources were adequately classified there seems every probability that schemes such as *Dewey* and *Library of Congress* could provide adequate access. We have seen how these schemes can be used for directories and catalogues but is it feasible that *all* electronic documents carried on the Internet could be classified in the same way as the items in a conventional library are classified, thus permitting a particular class number to be used by a search engine as the search criteria? In order to achieve this, the relevant classification information would need to be carried within the document itself. A proposed metadata (data about data) standard that could be used for this purpose is the Dublin Core, a system that facilitates the inclusion of tagged description and identification information within Web documents. This means that classification numbers from a scheme such as *Dewey* or *Library of Congress* could be added to the document, which could then be retrieved with a classification number search. Whilst this is therefore theoretically possible, the problem is one of number; there are many, many millions of electronic documents on the Net and the logistics are daunting.

Classification schemes as aids to searching

However, there is the possibility of using a general classification scheme such as *Dewey* or *Library of Congress* as an *aid* to searching. Machine-readable versions of *Dewey*[14] and *Library of Congress*[15] are available which could assist here and, if the complete scheme was considered to be too detailed, outlines of these schemes are available.

The *Library of Congress Classification* and *Library of Congress Subject Headings* have also been made available online over the Net. The *Library of Congress Classification Web: pilot test* is available from the Cataloging Distribution Service of LC.[16]

Both *Dewey* and *Library of Congress*, as the reader now knows, are *enumerative* schemes. One *faceted* classification based on modern theory, which has been advocated for use as an aid to searching is the *Broad System of Ordering (BSO)* (see page 36). The following description extracted from the BSO website[17] attempts to explain how the scheme might be used:

> For an Internet searcher who has exhausted keyword and hypertext link search methods and needs to search further the Broad System of Ordering (BSO) offers a subject contextual reference framework against which to plot a comprehensive and systematic search strategy. It is particularly useful in clarifying decision-making in searching for subjects which can be named only by phrases rather than single words.
>
> When your search question dives straight into the haystack and instantly retrieves the sought needle, then you don't need BSO. At other times searching in a large information store or network may all too readily bring the needle-in-haystack problem to mind. You may draw a blank or be presented with an offering which is not quite what you were looking for. At such times BSO could often help in suggesting alternative search approaches. Similarly, if you are not quite sure of the appropriate subject word to begin your subject search with, a glance at the index and systematic schedules of BSO could help to set you on your way.

As with *Library of Congress*, it is possible to consult the schedules of *BSO* online and it can also be obtained on disk. A further example of a scheme which is available over the Net is the *ACM Computing Classification System* (see page 48).[18]

Automatic classification

As noted above, for a classifier to sit down and classify all of the electronic documents that appear on the Internet in the same way as this might be done in a library or information service clearly is not feasible. However, is it possible to remove the human intellectual effort and allow the computer to assign documents to appropriate subject categories *automatically*? Whilst there do not appear to be any practical, 'real-life' examples of this at present, research into automatic classification has been going on for a considerable length of time. This research has assumed a far greater importance in recent years as the need to improve access to Internet resources has intensified. Internet users can often be irritated and frustrated by a search engine's tendency to produce a vast plethora of results from which relevant information has to be sifted. There is a growing number of projects which attempt to examine whether automatic classification can be used to improve this situation. One method used in a number of research projects, for instance, entails the statistical analysis of the way in which terms co-occur in documents. 'Documents that share the same frequently occurring keywords and concepts are usually relevant to the same queries. Clustering such documents together enables them to be retrieved more easily and helps to avoid the retrieval of irrelevant information.' This quote is taken from a paper (Jenkins, 2001) that discusses the advantages of classification and describes the automatic classifier that is being developed as part of the Wolverhampton UK Web Library referred to earlier in this chapter. In the United States, the OCLC Office of Research is undertaking the Scorpion[19] project, in which the primary focus is the building of tools for automatic subject recognition based on well-known schemes such as the *Dewey Decimal Classification*. A full explanation of these and the many other research projects in this area is outside the scope of an elementary text of this nature but there seems little doubt that automatic classification can have a part to play in the provision of Internet access.

Conclusion

Newton (2000) tells us that the deficiency of search engines has been noted by a number of authors. It appears that current engines are not efficient enough tools to provide adequate access to such an extended resource base as the Internet. 'The tendency of automated search engines to inundate users with irrelevant results has prompted reconsideration of the merits of classification.' It seems clear that there is a significant role for classification and, of course, as demonstrated in the previous chapter, *all* types of searching must involve classification to a certain degree.

Notes

1 Examples of Internet searching included in this chapter were valid at the time of writing in 2001.
2 Yahoo (www.yahoo.com) began as a simple directory of the favourite Web sites of two students. Although still probably best known as a search engine, it has now developed into a portal, or gateway, to the Internet offering other features such as news and online shopping.
3 http://www.excite.com
4 http://www.google.com
5 http://www.webrary.org/ref/weblinksmenu.html
6 http://www.scit.wlv.ac.uk/wwlib/
7 http://www.public.iastate.edu/~cyberstacks/homepage.html
8 http://www.scout.cs.wisc.edu/archives/
9 http://www.niss.ac.uk
10 http://ariadne.inf.fu-berlin.de:8000/
11 http://omni.ac.uk
12 http://www.sosig.org
13 http://conceptspace.lbs.ac.uk
14 A Microsoft Windows-based CD-ROM version of the 21st edition of Dewey was released shortly after the publication of the printed version and an update disk is issued annually.
15 *Classification Plus* is a full-text Windows based CD-ROM updated quarterly. *Library of Congress Subject Headings* are included.
16 http://classweb.loc.gov
17 http://www.classbso.demon.co.uk
18 http://www.informatik.uni-stuttgart.de
19 http://orc.rsch.oclc.org:6109

References

Dodd, David G. (1996), 'Grass roots cataloguing and classification: food for thought from World Wide Web subject-oriented lists', *Library Resources and Technical Services*, 40 (3), pp. 275-286.

Jenkins, Charlotte, *et al.* (2001), *Automatic Classification of Web Resources using Java and Dewey Decimal Classification*. Available on the Internet at: http://www7.scu.edu.au/programme/posters/1846/com1846.htm

MacLennan, Alan (2000), 'Classification and the Internet', in Rita Marcella and Arthur Maltby (eds), *The Future of Classification*, Gower, Aldershot, Hants; Burlington, VT, pp. 59-68.

Neely, Mark (1999), *All about searching the Internet*, rev. edn, Net.Works, Harrogate, Yorkshire, p. 17

Newton, Robert (2000), 'Information technology and new directions', in Rita Marcella and Arthur Maltby (eds), *The Future of Classification*, Gower, Aldershot, Hants; Burlington, VT, pp. 59-68.

Veltman, Chloe (2001), 'Right royal Google', *Daily Telegraph*, April 19.

16   Conclusion

This text has attempted to outline some of the ways in which classification can be used in information storage and retrieval. Hopefully it has succeeded in showing that classification must be considered a very useful tool for the organization and location of documents, records or data in an information system. Langridge (1973) states that in information work, 'classification is the basis for all index languages' and he emphasizes that 'there is no substitute'. Clifton (1994) maintains that 'coding' is an essential feature in computer-based business systems because 'it is impossible to identify, uniquely and unerringly, even as few as a thousand different entities if only their descriptions are available'.

No one classification scheme will be suitable for all purposes and the choice, or design, of a classification scheme will be governed by factors such as the type of information system, the objectives of the system, and user requirement. A public library, for example, will require a general scheme, covering the whole of recorded knowledge, and with special features such as a generalia class. For shelf arrangement, in a library of this nature, notational complexity should be avoided; not only is this confusing but lengthy numbers are inconvenient to inscribe on the spines of books or pamphlets.

A school library's requirement will be similar to that of the public library but there may well be a need for the classification to reflect the curriculum, that is the way that subjects are taught. Teachers sometimes criticize certain schemes from this point of view, the *Dewey Decimal Classification*, for instance, which distributes the subject 'Geography' through various classes: 380, 550, 910, and so on. The school library may therefore prefer some other scheme that, in its opinion, more closely adheres to the needs of library users. However, the *Library of Congress Classification* and the *Dewey Decimal Classification* are in widespread use in public libraries in the United States, the United Kingdom and elsewhere. A school library using one scheme and an adjacent public library using another is itself a situation which creates a further problem, namely a lack of standardization, which is hardly conducive to ease of use and customer satisfaction.

The smaller school library could of course consider a scheme such as *Dewey* too detailed and decide to look for something simpler. In fact, for this reason, abridged versions of schemes such as *Dewey* and the *Bliss Bibliographic Classification* have been compiled for use in school libraries.

Conversely, a special library, or information service, could find a general scheme not detailed enough. A perfume and cosmetics firm would discover that the *Dewey Decimal Classification* provides only four divisions for their particular subject area, that is:

668.5	Perfumes and cosmetics
668.54	Perfumes
668.542	Natural
668.544	Synthetic
668.55	Cosmetics

This would be completely inadequate; much greater specificity would be needed. A special scheme would have to be adopted or designed, although a general scheme might be used for peripheral subject areas. Table Q of *Uniclass* (see page 28), for example, consists of an outline of the *Universal Decimal Classification*. This 'indicates how *UDC* can be used to classify subjects not covered elsewhere in the *Uniclass* system' (Crawford, 1997, p. 13).

It may well be that choice is not possible because a classification scheme is already in use in a particular system and the cost of reclassification, even if warranted, would be prohibitive. If choice *is* possible, it could be that a certain scheme may be adopted because it is already in use elsewhere in a similar information environment and therefore is tried and tested. There are many existing classification schemes, both general and in a wide range of subject areas. If the use of classification is being considered for the first time, it could be advantageous to attempt to ascertain whether an appropriate scheme is already available.

It is also possible to incorporate the features of one scheme in another. The new edition of the *Bibliographic Classification* makes such use of other schemes, for example the *British Catalogue of Music Classification*, where appropriate. In the *London Classification of Business Studies*, Class P Law owes a great deal to *Classification Scheme for Law Books* by Elizabeth Moys and Class K Industries is adapted from the Central Statistical Office's *Standard Industrial Classification*. In turn, class C Management in *Uniclass* owes a debt to the *London Classification of Business Studies*.

Whether an existing classification is being considered or an original scheme is being compiled, attention must be paid to a number of the points that have been referred to throughout this text. For instance, decisions may need to be taken with regard to structure, citation order and notation.

A hierarchical structure might be chosen where it was desired to build in an expressive notation, so that superordinate, coordinate and subordinate relationships can be easily recognized from class numbers. Alternatively, where expressiveness was not so important, but flexibility and the ability to classify complex subjects were, the choice would probably be a faceted scheme. It is possible to make the notation expressive in a faceted scheme (see page 78) but only to a limited extent. The very nature of this type of scheme militates against expressiveness, especially when classification numbers for complex subjects can be built up by the combination of notations from various classes. It is easy to visualize 12 being a division of 1, or AB being a division of A, but how is the structure of the *CI/SfB Construction Indexing Manual* revealed by a number such as 81(24)Xf(J)? 'The brackets and the combinations of upper case and lower case letters made the codes difficult to understand. This complex notation also caused problems with computerisation' (Crawford, 1997, p. 9).

A citation order should be selected which will ensure that the scheme adheres as closely as possible to user needs. In a manual system the arrangement resulting from the citation order must be carefully considered. A certain filing order may suit the users of one information service but not another, and for this reason schemes such as *Uniclass,* the *London Education Classification* and the *London Classification of Business Studies* allow for flexibility and permit the adoption of a citation order which most closely caters for an information service's particular requirement. The latter scheme, for example, places the subject 'Organisation and methods and work study' at X, alphabetically one of the last classes. If a particular information system desires to collect everything on 'Organisation and work study' together, then Class X could be cited first rather than last. Thus 'Work study in the food industry' would be XE/KBA (where KBA = Food industry) rather than KBA/XE, and 'Work study in banks' would be XE/ECB (where ECB = Banks) rather than ECB/ XE.

Notation should be as brief and simple as possible. If specificity, that is the degree to which an exact subject may be specified, is required then lengthy notations may have to be accepted. If the notation is to be handled solely by a computer, length and complexity will not matter; only human beings become confused by complexity, not machines. However, for product coding in industry a fixed-length numeric notation may well be preferred, for example 2310, which, in the NATO codification system, indicates 'Passenger motor vehicles' (see also pages 74 to 76).

Searching is obviously facilitated in computerized systems if concepts are identified consistently by the same notation. In fixed-length class numbers, identification need not be unique but, if not unique, there must be positional consistency. For example, in the classification for machine bolts (page 25), a search for '2' in position one would be for 'brass' but in position four would be for 'chromium plated'. In other types of notation, uniqueness would be necessary. In *Uniclass*, the concept 'Women' is N5331 and this is the only number for that concept. In the *Library of Congress Classification*, the concept 'Women' is to be found in a great many enumerated subjects, in various classes and with differing notations, and it would be impossible to search for all the various aspects of this concept by class number. Clearly consistency is easier to achieve in a faceted scheme, although it does not always happen in practice. *Uniclass* itself often uses different notations for the one concept as is demonstrated by the extract from the index on page 30.

Decisions relating to structure, citation order and notation may be the only decisions required where a simple scheme for the coding of entities in a machine-based system is concerned. For more complex computer systems, and for other purposes, other factors must be taken into account. For detailed schemes an alphabetical index will be necessary and an explanatory introduction should be supplied.

Classification can aid the search procedure and, as explained in Chapters 13 to 15, alphabetical indexing techniques should be based upon classificatory principles. Computerized information systems are now the norm. The Internet has revolutionized the accessing of information. In the 1980s, it was forecast that there would be a move towards 'the refinement of the use of classification in machine systems' (Gorman, 1983) and that it was likely that classification would become mandatory in online searching' (Richmond, 1983). Whilst these forecasts have materialized only in part, 'Increasingly, local online systems and search engines are using hierarchical or classification-based browsers to organise and navigate Internet resources. This is a logical development, after all classification was devised in the beginning as a response to the need for organising large amounts of knowledge and information' (Chan, 2000).

To sum up, 'one of the major objectives of an information retrieval system is to allow the user to discover with the minimum of effort any items not relevant to an enquiry. Classification schemes set out to achieve this by grouping items according to specified characteristics'. Foskett (1982), however, from whose work this quote is taken, adds an important warning: 'provided that our specification meets the user's needs, this grouping will be helpful, but if it does not, our organisation of information may prove to be a positive hindrance instead of a help'. This is certainly a message to be heeded, classification is a means to an end, not an end in itself. Cutter (1904) had it right way back in the nineteenth century when he maintained that the ease of the user is to be preferred to that of the indexer.

References

Chan, Lois Mai and Hodges, Theodora L. (2000), 'The Library of Congress classification', in Rita Marcella and Arthur Maltby (eds), *The Future of Classification*, Gower, Aldershot, Hants; Burlington, VT, pp. 105-127.

Clifton, H.O. and Sutcliffe, A.G. (1994), *Business Information Systems*, 5th edn, Prentice Hall, New York; London, p. 320.

Crawford, Marshall, Cann, John and O'Leary, Ruth (eds) (1997), *Uniclass: Unified Classification for the Construction Industry*, RIBA, London, p. 13.

Cutter, Charles A. (1904), *Rules for a Dictionary Catalog*, 4th edn, Government Printing Office, Washington, p. 6.

Foskett, A.C. (1982), *The Subject Approach to Information*, 4th edn, Bingley, London, p. 158.

Gorman, Michael (1983), 'Technical services, 1984-2001 (and before)', *Technical Services Quarterly*, 1 (1/2), pp. 65-71.

Langridge, Derek (1973), *Approach to Classification for Students of Librarianship*, Bingley, London, p. 112.

Richmond, Phyllis A. (1983), 'Futuristic aspects of subject access', *Library Resources and Technical Services*, 27 (1), pp. 88-93.

Bibliography

This list contains entries for classification schemes and other monographic items referred to in the text, but a selection of other works on classification and related topics, which might be useful for further reading, has been added.

Mention should also be made of serials relevant to the subject. Notable examples are: *Cataloging and Classification Quarterly* (Haworth Press, Binghamton, NY); *Catalogue and Index* (Library Association Cataloguing and Indexing Group, quarterly); and *Knowledge Organisation* (formerly *International Classification*, the quarterly journal of the International Society for Knowledge Organisation). Other, less subject specific, serial publications such as *Library Resources and Technical Services* (Association for Library Collections and Technical Services, American Library Association, quarterly) may also contain articles and information that are of interest. In addition, the reader should note that the Internet is a veritable mine of information on the subject.

ACM Computing Classification System (1999), Association for Computing Machinery. Available on the Internet at http://www.informatik.uni-stuttgart.de/

Aitchison, Jean, Gilchrist, Alan and Bawden, Alan (1997), *Thesaurus Construction and Use: a Practical Manual*, 3rd edn, Aslib, London.

Aitchison, Jean, Gomersall, Alan and Ireland, Ralph (1969), *Thesaurofacet: a thesaurus and classification for engineering and related subjects*, 4th edn, English Electric, Leicester.

Austin, Derek and Dykstra, Mary (1984), *PRECIS: a manual of concept analysis and subject indexing*, 2nd edn, British Library, London.

Bakewell, K.G.B. (1978), *Classification and Indexing Practice*, Bingley, London.

Batty, David (1992), *An Introduction to the Twentieth Edition of the Dewey Decimal Classification*, Library Association, London.

Bengsten, Betty G. and Hill, Janet-Swan (eds.) (1990), *Classification of Library Materials: current and future potential for providing access*, Neal-Schuman, London, New York.

Bliss, H.E. (1940-53), *A Bibliographic Classification*, H.W. Wilson, New York, 4 v.

Bliss, H.E. (1977-), *Bliss Bibliographic Classification*, 2nd edn, Butterworths, London, vols in progress.

Booth, Pat F. and South, M.L. (1982), *Information Filing and Finding*, Elm Publications, Buckden, Cambs.

Bowker, Geoffrey C. and Star, Susan Leigh (1999), *Sorting Things Out: classification and its consequences*, MIT, Cambridge, Mass.

British Standards Institution (1987), *Guidelines for the Establishment and Development of Monolingual Thesauri*, 2nd edn, BSI, Milton Keynes. (BS 5723). Based upon the 'guidelines' previously issued by the International Standards Organisation (ISO 2788).

BSI Root Thesaurus (1988), 3rd edn, British Standards Institution, Milton Keynes.

BSO: Broad System of Ordering (1991), prepared by the FID/BSO Panel (Eric Coates, *et al.*), rev. edn. Machine-readable version (available on disk and on the Internet at www.classbso.demon.co.uk).   The copyright of BSO is now held by SLAIS (School of Library and Information Studies), University College, London, where responsibility for its future management now lies.

Buchanan, Brian (1979), *Theory of Library Classification*, Bingley, London.

Chan, Lois Mai (1990), *Library of Congress Subject Headings: principles and practice*, 3rd edn, Libraries Unlimited, Englewood, Co.

Chan, Lois Mai (1994), *Cataloging and Classification: an Introduction*, 2nd edn, McGraw Hill; New York.

Chan, Lois Mai (1999), *A Guide to the Library of Congress Classification*, Scarecrow Press, London.

Chan, Lois Mai, *et al.* (1996), *Dewey Decimal Classification: a practical guide*, 2nd edn, Forest Press, a Division of OCLC Online Computer Library Center, Albany, NY.

Clifton, H.O. and Sutcliffe, A.G. (1994), *Business Information Systems*, 5th edn, Prentice Hall, London; New York.

Coates, E.J. (1960), *The British Catalogue of Music Classification*, British National Bibliography, London.

Coates, E.J. (1960), *Subject Catalogues: Headings and Structure*, Library Association, London.

Comaromi, John, *et al.* (eds), *Abridged Dewey Decimal Classification and Relative Index*, 12th edn, Forest Press, a Division of OCLC Online Computer Library Center, Albany, NY.

Crawford, Marshall, Cann, John and O'Leary, Ruth (eds) (1997), *Uniclass: Unified Classification for the Construction Industry*, RIBA, London.

Cutter, Charles A. (1904), *Rules for a Dictionary Catalog*, 4th edn, Government Printing Office, Washington.

Defence Codification Agency (1997?), *Manufacturer's Guide to NATO Codification System*, The Agency, Glasgow.

Dewey, Melvil (1996), *Dewey Decimal Classification and Relative Index*, edition 21, ed. by Joan S. Mitchell, *et al.*, Forest Press, a Division of OCLC Online Computer Library Center, Albany, NY, 4 v.

Dittman, Helena (2000), *Learn Library of Congress Classification*, Scarecrow Press, London.

Downing, M.H. and Downing, D.H. (1992), *Introduction to Cataloguing and Classification*, 6th edn, McFarland, Jefferson, NC.

Drabenstott, K.M. and Vizine-Goetz, D. (1994), *Using Subject Headings for Online Retrieval: theory, practice and potential*, Academic Press, San Diego.

Ellis, David (1996), *Progress and Problems in Information Retrieval*, 2nd edn, Library Association, London.

Foskett, D.J. and Foskett, Joy (1974), *The London Education Classification: a thesaurus/classification of British educational terms*, 2nd edn, University of London, Institute of Education Library. Ongoing expansions and modifications are produced in-house.

Foskett, A.D. (1996), *The Subject Approach to Information*, 5th edn, Library Association, London.

Gilchrist, Alan and Strachan, David (eds) (1990), *The UDC: essays for a new decade*, Aslib, London.

Hildreth, Charles R. (1989), *The Online Catalogue: Developments and directions*, Library Association, London.

International Organization for Standardization (1986), *Documentation: Guidelines for the establishment and development of monolingual thesauri*, 2nd edn, The Organization, Geneva (ISO 2788).

Lancaster, F.W. (1998), *Indexing and Abstracting in Theory and Practice*, 2nd edn, Library Association, London.

Langridge, Derek (1973), *Approach to Classification for Students of Librarianship*, Bingley, London.

Langridge, Derek (1992), *Classification: Its kinds, systems, elements and applications*, Bowker-Saur, London.

Library of Congress (various dates), *Classification*, LC, Washington, 41 v. The examples included here have been checked in 2001 against *The Library of Congress classification web: pilot test*, available from the Cataloging Distribution Service of LC at http://classweb.loc.gov

Library of Congress Subject Headings (1995), 18th edn, LC, Washington. Also available on *Classification Plus*, a Windows-based CD-ROM. The examples included here have been checked in 2001 against *The Library of Congress classification web: pilot test*, available from the Cataloging Distribution Service of LC at http://classweb.loc.gov

London Business School Library (2000), *London Classification of Business Studies*, The Library, 2 v. This is a new version of the scheme first devised by K.D.C. Vernon and Valerie Lang in 1970, revised by K.G.B. Bakewell and David Cotton in 1979.

MacConnell, W. (1971), *Classification and Coding: an introduction and review of classification and coding systems*, British Institute of Management, London.

Maltby, Arthur (1975), *Sayers' Manual of Classification for Librarians*, 5th edn, Deutsch, London, p. 61. Marcella (1994) is essentially a revised edition of this manual.

Marcella, Rita and Maltby, Arthur (eds) (2000), *The Future of Classification*, Gower, Aldershot, Hants; Burlington, VT.

Marcella, Rita and Newton, Robert (1994), *A New Manual of Classification*, Gower, Aldershot, Hants; Burlington, VT. Essentially a revised edition of Maltby (1975).

McIlaine, I.C., with participation from A. Buxton (1993), *Guide to the Use of the UDC*, International Federation for Information and Documentation, The Hague. FID occasional paper, 5.

Neely, Mark (1999), *All About Searching the Internet*, rev edn, Net.Works, Harrogate, Yorks.

Orna, E. (1983), *Build Yourself a Thesaurus: a step-by-step guide*, Running Angel, Norwich.

Ranganathan, S.R. (1987), *Colon Classification,* 7th edn, edited by M.A. Gopinath, Sarada Ranganathan Endowment for Library Science, Bangalore.

Ray-Jones, Alan and Clegg, David (1991), *CI/SfB Construction Indexing Manual,* RIBA, London. Abridged reprint of 1976 revision.

RCN Library Nursing Thesaurus: a thesaurus of terms used in nursing, midwifery, health visiting and related subject areas (1998), 3rd edn, RCN [Royal College of Nursing] Library and Information Services, London.

Rowley, Jennifer (1996), *The Basics of Information Systems,* 2nd edn, Library Association, London.

Rowley, Jennifer and Farrow, John (2000), *Organizing Knowledge: an Introduction to Managing Access to Information,* 3rd edn, Gower, Aldershot, Hants; Burlington, VT.

Scott, Mona L. (1998), *Dewey Decimal Classification: a study manual and number building guide,* Libraries Unlimited, Englewood, Colo.

Shaw, Josephine (1984), *Administration for Business,* 2nd edn, Pitman, London.

Smith, Raymond (1966), *Classification for London Literature based upon the Collection in the Guildhall Library,* 3rd edn, The Library Committee, London. Cited in George A. Carter (1973), *J.L. Hobbs's Local History and the Library,* 2nd rev. edn, Deutsch, London.

Soergel, Dagobert (1974), *Indexing Languages and Thesauri: construction and maintenance,* Melville, Los Angeles.

Soergel, Dagobert (1985), *Organising Information: principles of database and retrieval systems,* Academic Press, Orlando, Florida; London.

Thesaurus of Psychological Index Terms (1997), 8th edn, edited by Alvin Walker, Jr, American Psychological Association, Washington, DC.

Thomas, A.R. (ed.) (1995), *Classification: options and opportunities,* Haworth, New York. Also published as *Cataloging and Classification Quarterly,* 19 (3/4).

Unesco Thesaurus: a structured list of descriptors for indexing and retrieving literature in the fields of education, science, culture, communication and information (1994), New edn, Unesco, Paris. Previous edition compiled by Jean Aitchison, 1977.

Universal Decimal Classification (1993), International medium edn, English text, Edition 2 British Standards Institution, Milton Keynes, 2v. (BS 1000M:1993).

Vickery, B.C. (1960), *Faceted Classification: a guide to construction and use of special schemes,* Aslib, London.

Viet, Jean and Slype, Georges van (1984), *EUDISED Multilingual Thesaurus for Information Processing in the Field of Education,* New edn, English version, Mouton, Berlin. At head of title: Council of Europe. Commission of the European Communities.

Winslade, B.A.J. (1986), *Dewey Decimal Classification for School Libraries,* British and International edn, edited by Mary L. South, Forest Press, Albany, NY. Originally published as: 'Introduction to the *Dewey Decimal Classification* for British schools'.

Index